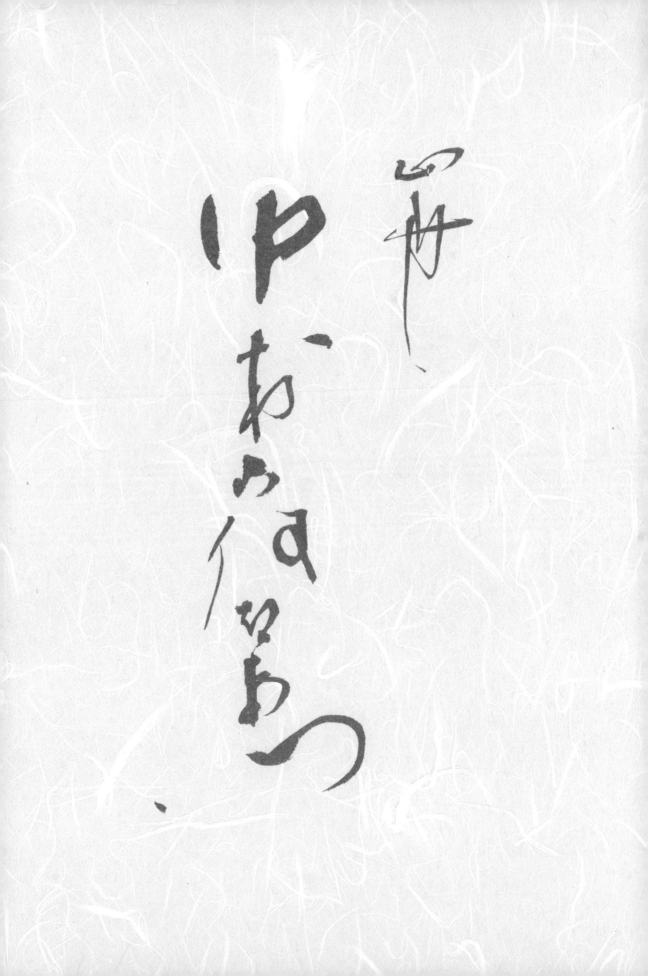

四世

Nakamura Jakuemon IV
The Art of *Onnagata* Acting

中村雀右衛門

笹口玲

Jo Barbara Massey,

Rei Sasaguchi

May 31, 2008

CONTENTS

ILLUSTRATIONS

Plate 1. Nakamura Jakuemon putting on
his stage makeup at the Kabukiza

Photograph by Yutaka Umemura

Plate 2. The late Matsumoto Hakuō as Narukami (left)
and Nakamura Jakuemon as Taemahime
in *"Narukami"*
(Kabukiza, July 1978)

Photograph by Yutaka Umemura

Plate 3. Nakamura Jakuemon as Chiyo in "*Terakoya*"
(Kabukiza, March 2000)

Photograph by Yutaka Umemura

Plate 4. Kataoka Nizaemon as Chūbei (behind) and
Nakamura Jakuemon as Umegawa prepare
to flee in *Koibikyaku Yamato Ōrai*
(National Theater, April 1983)

Photograph by Yutaka Umemura

Plate 5. Nakamura Jakuemon as Hanako
in the guise of a priestess dancing
the introductory passage of *"Musume Dōjōji"*
(Imperial Theater, December 1974)

Photograph by Yutaka Umemura

Preface

I first saw the actor Nakamura Jakuemon, whose real name is Seiji Aoki, in the early summer of 1986 when I interviewed him at the Kabukiza Theater in Tokyo for my column in *The Japan Times*. Jakuemon was then sixty-five years old and at the peak of his career as one of Kabuki's foremost *onnagata* (actors performing female roles). After that interview, I was unable to meet up with Jakuemon for years, kept busy by work commitments at the Idemitsu Museum of Art, Tokyo, where I was a research fellow from 1987 to 1996. When I saw Jakuemon again in the fall of 1999, I was astounded—at the age of seventy-eight, the actor looked as young and vigorous as he had been thirteen years earlier! During more than a decade, in which I never saw Jakuemon offstage, the actor was designated a *Ningen Kokuhō* (Living National Treasure), an honor he received in 1991.

Soon after renewing my association with Jakuemon, I hit upon the idea of writing about him and his beloved Kabuki—which I have followed for twenty years. Receiving his enthusiastic endorsement, I have, for the past three years, been visiting Jakuemon in his dressing room behind the Kabukiza a few times a month, to hear his thoughts on the different roles he was playing that month and to watch him work on his makeup while seated at his elegant dressing table. The aim of this small volume is to share with readers my precious experience of receiving lessons on Kabuki from the most eminent *onnagata* active today.

My interest in Jakuemon was piqued by the fact that he decided to become an *onnagata* relatively late in his career, yet succeeded in becoming an excellent one. Originally brought up by his actor father Ōtani Tomoemon VI, to become a *tachiyaku* (male lead), Jakuemon began to tackle the formidable range of skills required by an *onnagata* at the age of twenty-seven, after serving in the army for six years during World War II. His efforts received the support and backing of Matsumoto Kōshirō VII (1870-1949), one of the most influential Kabuki actors of postwar Japan. Jakuemon rose to the late Kōshirō's expectations, becoming a fully-fledged *onnagata* in thirty years. He has reigned over the Kabuki world ever since.

As a key to understanding the nature of Jakuemon's *onnagata* art and the extent of his accomplishments, I would like to present here an account of the early history of Kabuki, one of Japan's traditional theatrical forms, from its birth (under the name of Kabuki Odori) at the beginning of the 17th century to the emergence of the *onnagata* —actors specializing in female roles—around the middle of that century. *Onnagata* came into existence when the young performers who wore their hair in the *wakashu* style were ousted from the field of Kabuki Odori entertainment in 1652. Kabuki began to develop thereafter as an independent theatrical form during the second half of the 17th century.

The techniques of portraying courtesans and other women were developed by pioneering *onnagata* actors, and by the middle of the 18th century *onnagata* technique had been formulated by such talented actors as Yoshizawa Ayame and Segawa Kikunojō. The *kata* (patterns) of *onnagata* acting they devised continued to be used by their followers in the succeeding centuries. The patterns were then re-evaluated and refined by Nakamura Utaemon V and his son Utaemon VI during the last century, and from Utaemon VI, transmitted directly to Nakamura Jakuemon.

Nakamura Utaemon VI (1917-2001), the most distinguished *onnagata* of the 20th century, was instrumental in Jakuemon's formation as an *onnagata* because the younger actor learned not only the general techniques of *onnagata* acting from him, but also the specific ways of performing many key roles. These included the famous heroines of *jidaimono* (historical plays), which exemplify the stylized beauty of Kabuki adapted from Bunraku plays. The most notable of the *jidaimono* roles that Jakuemon mastered under the late Utaemon are Tokihime in "*Kamakura Sandaiki* (Records of the Three Generations of the Kamakura Shogunate)," Yukihime in "*Kinkakuji* (The Golden Pavilion)" and Yaegakihime in "*Honchō Nijūshikō* (The Twenty-four Models of Filial Piety: The Japanese Version)."

For Jakuemon, the performance of an *onnagata* role is a process of crystallizing femininity into a form of highly restrained beauty, a process in which the actor feels enormously constrained and tense. Over the past ten years, since Utaemon VI retired from the Kabuki stage in 1993, Jakuemon, while carefully adhering to the *kata* he inherited from his mentor, has introduced distinctive styles to his performances. And whether the role is from a well-known *jidaimono*, or a dance drama, Jakuemon's performance is the fruit of his perseverance over half a century — enhanced by his lovely sensual figure. While carrying on the legacy of Utaemon, Jakuemon's performances are now uniquely his own: His women smoulder within and bubble with the magma of passion, differing from the cool, ethereal beauty of the late Utaemon.

When performing the role of a married woman, such as Sagami, the wife of the gallant protagonist Naozane in "*Kumagai Jin'ya* (Kumagai's Camp)," or Chiyo, the wife of Matsuōmaru in the scene known as "*Terakoya* (Temple School)" from "*Sugawara Denju Tenarai Kagami* (Sugawara Certifies a Disowned Disciple to Perpetuate his Line of Calligraphy)," the *onnagata* has to repress his emotions and behavior toward the *tachiyaku* playing the part of the husband. The *onnagata* must adjust his performance according to that of the *tachiyaku*; he must also pay his acting partner due respect, especially when the *tachiyaku* is younger than himself. (Over the past few decades, Jakuemon has frequently played opposite his nephews — Ichikawa Danjūrō, Matsumoto Kōshirō and Nakamura Kichiemon.) Only in "*Kinkakuji*," or in the final scene of "*Imoseyama Onna Teikin* (Admonitions to Women on Their Relationship With Men)," can the *onnagata*, freed from psychological fetters, perform Yukihime or Omiwa alone, revealing the ardor of each woman for her beloved.

Various facets of Jakuemon's art are illustrated beautifully in the photographs taken by Yutaka Umemura over the past thirty years. To help the reader better appreciate Jakuemon's art, photographs of various plays and dance numbers from Jakuemon's repertory are presented in the second part of this volume, accompanied by synopses of the stories.

I   The Birth of Kabuki

Kabuki, like Japan's other traditional theatrical genres, is now performed exclusively by men. The birth of Kabuki, however, is traced back to a woman known as Okuni, one of the numerous itinerant female entertainers who were active in 16th-century Japan. Although Okuni is generally credited with being the originator of Kabuki, what she started four centuries ago was a type of entertainment called Kabuki[1] Odori[2] or the "exotic dance"—rather different from the Kabuki theater as we know it today.

Okuni is mentioned in the *Tōdaiki* (Records of Happenings in Contemporary Times), compiled in the early 17th century. According to the *Tōdaiki*, Okuni presented her first Kabuki Odori in the precincts of the Kitano Tenman Shrine in Kyoto in the fourth month of the eighth year of Keichō (1603), the year in which Tokugawa Ieyasu established the Tokugawa shogunate. Okuni is referred to as "Okuni, a priestess from Izumo Province (Shimane Prefecture)," but the question of whether she actually came from Izumo has not been proved.[3] We can imagine that Okuni perhaps claimed to be from Izumo for romantic effect, or maybe she even posed as a priestess to collect money on the pretext of fundraising for the Grand Shrine at Izumo.

In her Kabuki Odori performance given at the Kitano Tenman Shrine that spring, Okuni made her appearance as a dashing young samurai, wearing an exotic but fashionable outfit that revealed some *namban*[4] influence. As a young man of "strikingly unusual" appearance, her character drops in at a teahouse in town and dallies with its proprietress (a role probably performed by a Kyōgen actor). After drinking together, the dandy dances by himself and with the proprietress of the teahouse. Okuni's Kabuki Odori was applauded by the townspeople of Kyoto as an exciting new form of entertainment. Her reputation rose so quickly that the following month she was invited by Konoe Sakiko, the consort of Emperor Goyōzei (r. 1586-1611), to perform Kabuki Odori at the imperial palace for the emperor's mother, Shin Jōtōmon'in,[5] who is known to have patronized various forms of performing arts.

The trend for *kabuku* (meaning "to be out of the ordinary") began among young members of the local warrior families in the 1570s, a time when the famous warlord (and extravagant dresser) Oda Nobunaga rose to power. After the assassination of Nobunaga in 1582, the trend continued to thrive under Toyotomi Hideyoshi, one of Nobunaga's vassals who, upon his master's death, seized control over the country. And it lingered even after the death of Hideyoshi in 1598, remaining popular among young samurai and noblemen at the court of Emperor Goyōzei until the downfall of Hideyoshi's heir, Hideyori, in 1615. Okuni's daring Kabuki Odori at the Kitano Shrine caused a sensation precisely because she put on the stage the trendsetting young men of the moment, dressed in their Kabuki fashion.

Long before attaining fame, Okuni was known to the aristocratic circles in Kyoto as the performer of Yayako Odori,[6] *yayako* meaning "baby" or "infant." Attempts have been made by scholars to trace Okuni's background by referring to diaries written in the last quarter of the 16th century.[7] Okuni may be identified with one of the two girls performing Yayako Odori mentioned in two contemporary diaries, *Oyudono no ue no Nikki*, recorded in the ninth month of the ninth year of Tenshō (1581), and *Tamon'in Nikki*, recorded in the 10th year of Tenshō (1582). In *Tamon'in Nikki*, Tamon'in Eishun of the Kōfukuji Temple in Nara writes on the 18th day of the fifth month in 1582 that "The girls aged eight and eleven from Kaga Province (Ishikawa Prefecture) gave a performance of Yayako Odori, also called Kaga Odori, at the Wakamiya of the Kasuga Shrine in Nara."[8] It is possible to surmise from these records that twenty years before Okuni gave her 1603 Kabuki Odori performance, she was making a living by performing Yayako Odori, or perhaps belonged to a small troupe of entertainers with Yayako Odori in their repertory. Okuni is thought also to have had Nembutsu Odori (performed while reciting the name of the Buddha Amitābha)[9] in her repertory, as there is pictorial evidence in the Yamato Bunkakan[10] in Nara.

The Yayako Odori consists of a set of dances, such as Oharagi Odori and Hinda Odori, performed by two or three girls around the same age. The girls dance as they sing popular love songs called *kouta*, punctuated by refrains. Their graceful movements are similar to those of the traditional *mai* dance, but the dancers turn lively and rhythmical when the refrain comes. During the Yayako Odori performances, a *dōke* (jester) referred to as Saruwaka would appear to enliven proceedings with his simple, comical mimicry.[11] The Yayako Odori has been preserved under the name of "Ayako Mai" in the areas of Shimono and Takaharada in Kashiwazaki, Niigata Prefecture. Interestingly, the Ayako Mai seems to retain elements of Okuni's Kabuki Odori, as it consists of a set of *kouta* dances performed by two or three girls to the accompaniment of a flute and drums, and some Kyōgen numbers performed by men.

1.   Men and women performing Furyū Odori in the garden of a sumptuous Kyoto residence (right-hand screen of pair of sixfold screens; datable to the 1630s)
     Courtesy of Idemitsu Bijutsukan, Tokyo

The Kabuki Odori and the Yayako Odori were both born out of the tradition of Furyū Odori, which had evolved from the Buddhist Bon Odori. The Bon dances were simple affairs performed by men and women in towns and farming areas to the accompaniment of handbells and drums at the *ullambana* festival in the middle of July or August, a time when the spirits of the dead are believed to be reunited with their families. The Bon Odori, danced in groups at the end of the festival to send ancestral spirits back to the other world, had been popular in the countryside since the last quarter of the 15th century.

The practice of Furyū Odori became widespread from around 1520 and its popularity peaked in the mid-16th century, supported by the rising prosperity of the merchant classes in the region covering Kyoto and Osaka, referred to as *kamigata*. During the 1520s, a frenzy for Furyū dance overtook the aristocratic circles in Kyoto, and nobles

soon began to compete with townsfolk not only in the scale of their dance events but also in the elaborate ornamentation of their costumes and accessories,[12] such as the lavishly decorated parasols and standards occupying the center of each circle of the dance. Although the Furyū Odori was performed in the open (fig. 1), Okuni put her Kabuki Odori on a platform, borrowing the type of stage used for Nō and Kyōgen performances.

If one of the girls dancing the Yayako Odori recorded in *Tamon'in Nikki* in 1582 really was Okuni, she would have been almost thirty years old at the time of her Kabuki Odori. Being somewhat plain-looking,[13] it was necessary for Okuni to appear well made-up, but she was nonetheless bold enough to appear in the title role as a Kabuki dandy, the object of adoration in Kyoto at the time. Perhaps one reason for the acclaim she received was that it reflected the pleasure-loving atmosphere of Kyoto at the turn of the 17th century. What's more, though assuming the form of a man onstage, Okuni, a woman approaching middle-age and doubtless with ample life experience, would surely have imparted a kind of sensuality even though her body was hidden under the exotic men's attire she wore.

The form of entertainment Okuni staged in Kyoto in the spring of 1603 was not merely a novel form of dance, since the main feature of *odori* was preceded by a skit in which Okuni also performed the *shite* (principal character). Her character, the fashionably dressed young man, makes advances toward a teahouse proprietress, using provocative words and gestures. After the two drink together, the Kabuki Odori climaxes with a set of dances performed by the guest, the proprietress and the jester. They sing some *kouta* songs and dance, together and singly, to the accompaniment of a flute and hand drums. In her creation of this scene, Okuni owed a debt to the realistic, comical Kyōgen theater, which, like the Nō theater, had fully developed long before Okuni emerged on the scene.

During the 16th and 17th centuries, Kyōgen was popular generally among the ordinary people, while the elegantly stylized Nō theater was favored by aristocrats or those of the power-hungry warlord class.[14] It is conceivable that Okuni was associated with a group of local Kyōgen actors who did not belong to any of the major Nō or Sarugaku troupes.[15] She may have learned from them the technique of performing the type of Kyōgen plays[16] in which the principal character invites several men and women called *tachishū* to drink together and present *komai*[17] dances in turn.

In a great many Nō plays, heroes from the other world appear on the stage, hiding their faces with masks. Breaking away from the Nō tradition, Okuni presented a scene from contemporary life and used the structure of Kyōgen plays to tell the story of a stylish young man seeking pleasure in a teahouse. The idea of applying genre scenes to the stage and of incorporating dance remained important in the Kabuki theater as it developed in subsequent centuries. Also, elements of drama found in the simple skit in Okuni's Kabuki Odori evolved, during the 1650s, into Kabuki plays portraying men having fun with courtesans in the pleasure quarters.

There are a considerable number of screen-paintings dating from the first half of the 17th century that demonstrate the popularity of the Kabuki Odori staged by Okuni and by her followers. One of the earliest and finest examples is a pair of sixfold screens in the Idemitsu Museum of Art in Tokyo, attributed to the Hasegawa School (fig. 2). In the upper right-hand corner of the left screen is the Kitano Tenman Shrine in Kyoto with its characteristic *gongen*-style roof, and in the foreground are such flowers of the four seasons as chrysanthemum, camellia and *hagi* (Japanese bush clover). On the left of the screen, under a few cherry trees in full bloom, is a stage about four meters square, resembling a Nō stage. The stage has a gabled wooden roof and under the eaves on three of its sides hangs a narrow red curtain, while the back of the stage and the *hashigakari* (bridge) are covered with a tapestry striped in blue and gold. In the center of the stage stands the *shite*, her arms crossed in front of her, wearing a brown kimono under a black jacket and carrying two swords at her left hip. Here, Okuni poses in the title role of her Kabuki Odori. She has a *kidoku* hood over her hair, which is worn in the men's style, and the lower half of her face is covered with a piece of white cloth.[18]

In front of the *shite* sits a Kyōgen player, acting the role of the teahouse proprietress. He wears a red kimono and his hair is wrapped in a piece of white cloth. He hides his mouth behind a fan with the motif of a red sun on a white background, which he holds in his right hand. To the right of the two characters is Saruwaka, the jester, who here looks like a servant. With his face wrapped in a towel, Saruwaka appears to be teasing the young samurai and the woman of the teahouse. At the rear of the stage sit three musicians, playing a *taiko* drum and two *tsuzumi* drums of different sizes. About a dozen spectators are shown sitting or standing on the ground before the stage.

Okuni is known to have given Kabuki Odori performances at the

2.　Okuni gives her Kabuki Odori performance at the Kitano Tenman Shrine in Kyoto (left-hand screen of pair of sixfold screens; datable to the early 17th century)
Courtesy of Idemitsu Bijutsukan, Tokyo

Kitano Tenman Shrine in Kyoto from the fourth month of the eighth year of Keichō (1603) through the first month of the following year. Four years later, she left Kyoto to take her troupe on tour. When Okuni returned to Kyoto in 1612, at the age of forty, she is recorded as having once again given performances at the Kitano Shrine.[19] On that occasion, she presented a new Kabuki Odori featuring a Kabuki dandy who appears to have just come out of a public bathhouse — his hair tied with a towel as if it had just been washed.[20] Although Okuni's first Kabuki Odori had been hailed as a sensation in 1603, she clearly had to think of something new to attract audiences on her return to Kyoto nine years later.

The first thirty years of Okuni's life unfolded in the last quarter

of the 16th century, known as the Momoyama Era. She was a child when Oda Nobunaga rose to power after subduing rival warlords. Okuni is thought to have been about ten years old when Nobunaga was assassinated in 1582. From 1583 to 1598, when his vassal Toyotomi Hideyoshi held power, she was very active in the field of entertainment, performing Yayako Odori. And in 1603, five years after the death of Hideyoshi and the year in which Tokugawa Ieyasu was appointed shogun, Okuni, who was by then a seasoned entertainer, seized the limelight. Okuni's emergence as the originator of Kabuki Odori coincides with the period of transition during which the power of Hideyoshi's heir, Hideyori, declined rapidly as Tokugawa Ieyasu took control of the country.

The Kabuki Odori was a product of Okuni's unique background and her astute business sense. A child of the Momoyama Era, Okuni's Kabuki Odori was the last spark of that vibrant age. Between the death of Toyotomi Hideyoshi in 1598 and the establishment of the Tokugawa shogunate in 1603, the people were in turmoil, feeling a keen insecurity even though they had been freed from the fetters of Japan's medieval past. During the Keichō Era (1596-1615), the power of the *machishū* (merchants) in the *kamigata* region increased enormously and with their economic resources, they responded enthusiastically to new forms of entertainment, such as the Kabuki Odori.

Okuni disappeared from the entertainment scene in Kyoto a few years before the downfall of Toyotomi Hideyori in 1615, and the Kabuki Odori she had created passed into the hands of her followers. Yet the spirit of Okuni's Kabuki Odori, based on the tradition of performing arts native to Japan, survived in the form of the Kabuki theater throughout the 260 years of the Tokugawa regime, withstanding the waves of repression imposed by the authorities.

Notes

1. The term "Kabuki" derives from the verb *kabuku* meaning "to be slanted," "to wear exotic costume" or "to be out of the ordinary." *Kabuita* means "outlandish" and "strikingly unusual in color or design."

2. The Japanese term *odori*, meaning "dance," is used throughout this book, while *mai*, the type of dance popular in medieval Japan, is also translated as "dance." Performed usually by a person ruling or representing a community, *mai* is characterized by deliberate gliding or circling movements. *Odori*, which became popular in the 16th and early 17th centuries, was performed by a group or groups of people and featured lively, rhythmic or jumping movements, accompanied by the clapping of hands. The Japanese characters for *mai* and *odori* combined become *buyō*, and *buyō* may be performed onstage by a single person.

3. Tatsusaburō Hayashiya thinks that Okuni, when she was young, must have been a member of a local troupe of actors belonging to the Kōfukuji Temple in Nara. "Izumo no Okuni," *Chūsei Bunka no Kichō*, Tokyo · Daigaku Shuppankai, 1966, p. 294. Kyōko Ogasawara maintains that Okuni was a member of a troupe of actors originating in Kyoto or its vicinity. *Izumo no Okuni*, Tokyo · Chūkō Shinsho No. 734, 1984, p. 13.

4. *Namban* is the appellation given to the Portuguese who came to Japan for trade in the second half of the 16th century.

5. Recorded by nobleman Funabashi Hidekata in his diary, *Keichō Jikkenroku*, on the sixth day of the fifth month in the eighth year of Keichō (1603).

6. It is recorded in *Tokiyoshikyōki* in the fifth year of Keichō (1600) that the Yayako Odori from Izumo Province was presented at the Konoe residence on the first day of the seventh month. One of the dancers was called Kuni and the other, Kiku. Besides these two, there were about ten people in the troupe.

7. Hayashiya, *op. cit.*, p. 293; Hattori, Yukio. "Yayako Odori Kō," *Kabuki Seiritsu no Kenkyū*, Tokyo · Kazama Shobō, 1968, pp. 145-168; Ogasa-wara, Kyōko. *Kabuki no Tanjō*, Tokyo · Meiji Shoin, 1972, and *Izumo no Okuni*, Tokyo · Chūkō Shinsho No. 734, 1984.

8. The copies of *Tamon'in Nikki* have been preserved at Kōfukuji Temple in Nara.

9. Amitābha Buddha is called Amida Butsu in Japan.

10. *Selected Catalogue of the Museum Yamato Bunkakan* (Third Edition), Nara, 1970, pl. 21-1 (A section of "Okuni Kabuki Scroll").

11. The "*Kabuki Zukan*" in the Tokugawa Museum in Nagoya depicts several Yayako Odori numbers performed to *kouta* songs, crowned with the scene portraying a Kabuki dandy. *Kabuki Zukan*, Tokyo · Chūnichi Shimbun Shuppankyoku, 1964.

12. The most extravagant Furyū event was held at the Hōkoku Shrine in Kyoto in 1604 to commemorate the sixth anniversary of Toyotomi Hideyoshi's death in 1598.

13. It is mentioned in a footnote to the *Tōdaiki* that Okuni was "not so good-looking."

14. During the Tokugawa Period (1603-1867), the Nō theater was officially patronized by the shogunate.

15. Okuni's father or possibly husband, working as her promoter, may have been a Kyōgen actor.

16. "*Wakana*" and "*Kirokuda*" are excellent examples of such Kyōgen plays.

17. Short pieces of *mai* dance performed in certain Kyōgen plays.

18. Here, the *shite* — probably Okuni — hides her face to conceal her real age, or to parody the use of masks in Nō plays.

19. *Kitano Shake Nikki*, Vol. 6, Tokyo · Zoku Gunshoruijū Kanseikai, 1973, p. 203.

20. Excellent pictorial evidence of Okuni's new Kabuki Odori is found in a pair of screen-paintings in the Idemitsu Museum of Art. *Fūzokuga* (Catalogue of Japanese Genre Paintings in the Idemitsu Collection), Tokyo · Idemitsu Bijutsukan, 1987, pl. 16-1, 2.

II Women's Kabuki and Young Men's Kabuki

As the reputation of Okuni's 1603 Kabuki Odori performances at the Kitano Tenman Shrine spread across the country, numerous groups of women engaged in various forms of entertainment, such as Nō[1] or Kusemai,[2] began to follow in Okuni's footsteps. For two decades after Okuni's initial Kabuki Odori, her followers staged the dance at different sites in and around Kyoto; particularly spectacular were the performances given at outdoor theaters on the Kamo riverbed at Shijō.[3] Performances of Women's Kabuki Odori were presented on a grand scale by sumptuously dressed young women, forming a circle around a person playing the samisen,[4] a three-stringed musical instrument that began to be used for Kabuki Odori performances in the 1610s.

Scenes of Kabuki Odori being performed in outdoor theaters on the Kamo riverbed at Shijō are depicted in a great many screen-paintings of early-Edo date (fig. 3). These paintings emphasize the scale of the revue-like dances performed by handsome young women, most of whom were prostitutes. In these paintings, the skit in which the dashing Kabuki dandy takes the title role is less frequently represented, although the *dōke* (jester) is often included. In 1617, seven theaters were given permission to operate on the Kamo riverbed at Shijō under the protective policy of the Tokugawa shogunate. There they flourished through the Genroku Era (1688-1704), together with the neighboring pleasure quarters at Gion and Pontochō. The number of Kabuki theaters in Kyoto varied during the 18th and 19th centuries, but when the street of Shijō was expanded in 1893, only one theater was retained on the south side; it was named Minamiza, meaning South Theater.

The grandiose renditions of Kabuki Odori given on the Kamo riverbed were generally sponsored by the owners of brothels, their purpose being to display young women to prospective clients. In the 10th month of the sixth year of Kan'ei (1629), a quarter of a century after Okuni's initial performance of Kabuki Odori at the Kitano

Tenman Shrine, the Tokugawa authorities forbade the public appearance of female entertainers not only in Kabuki Odori, but also in Nō plays and *ningyō jōruri* (puppet shows). The ban did not mean the end of Kabuki Odori. As soon as women were forced to retreat from public entertainment in 1629, they were replaced by groups of good-looking boys and young men with *wakashu*-style hairdos that left their forelocks unshaven. These young people, called *wakashu*, began to vie with one another in performing Kabuki Odori. Such performances enjoyed considerable popularity until they, too, were prohibited by the Tokugawa authorities in 1652.

Troupes of boys and young men trained in Kyōgen and Kō-wakamai[5] had already been in existence around the turn of the 17th century, but they were overshadowed by the emergence of Okuni in 1603 and by her imitators in the following few decades. While Women's Kabuki was in vogue, the designation of Wakashu Kabuki (Young Men's Kabuki) was not used; instead such terms as Dōnan Kabuki or Warabe Kabuki were employed to designate Kabuki Odori as performed by boys.[6] As soon as Women's Kabuki was banned, however, those teenage male entertainers quickly added Kabuki Odori to their repertory, and began to stage Kabuki Odori performances of their own.

The nature of the performances staged by Wakashu Kabuki troupes has not been clarified satisfactorily due to the scarcity of written material.[7] We are certain, however, that the Young Men's Kabuki Odori did not differ greatly from the Women's Kabuki Odori, in which the star performer was judged mainly on his looks and his singing voice. The main feature of the Kabuki Odori was the sensual dance performed by the star to the accompaniment of *kouta* songs, samisen, flute, drum and hand drums. In addition to the *kouta* dances, Wakashu Kabuki troupes adopted elements of the Nō and Kyōgen theaters, Kōwakamai dances and acrobatic skills (referred to as *hōka*) to enrich their performances.

In creating her Kabuki Odori in 1603, Okuni borrowed the form of Kyōgen plays featuring drinking scenes and *komai* dances, but the

30

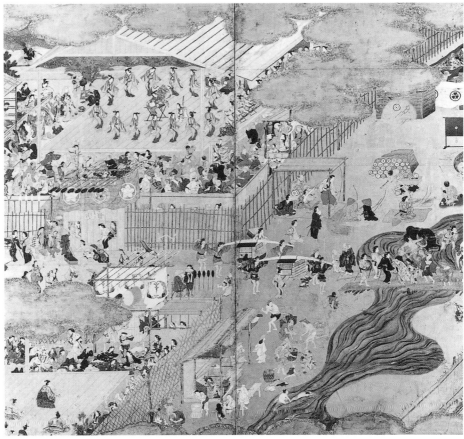

3.   Women's Kabuki Odori performance given on the Kamo riverbed at Shijō
      in Kyoto (left-hand screen of pair of twofold screens; datable to the 1620s)
      Courtesy of Seikadō Bunko Bijutsukan, Tokyo

influence of the Kyōgen theater is even more pronounced in the
performances of the Young Men's Kabuki. Following in the footsteps
of Okuni, members of the Young Men's Kabuki troupes adopted the
plot of a Kyōgen play with a drinking scene, and added *kouta* songs
and *komai* dances to showcase the beauty of participants. The fact that
some performers of the Young Men's Kabuki came from Nō or Kyōgen
backgrounds[8] accounts for the inclusion of more Kyōgen elements in
this version of the Kabuki Odori.

The Young Men's Kabuki Odori was established within the
tradition of *odori* and *mai*, as was the earlier Dōnan Kabuki performed by boys in the first quarter of the 17th century. The *mai*, or
komai, borrowed from the Kyōgen theater, was recognized as so
important that *wakashu* performers soon began to vie with one

another in gaining greater skill in the *mai* dance. Also in the Young Men's Kabuki, the simple form of *monomane* (mimicry) was used, specifically by the jester Saruwaka, who had enjoyed only a supporting role in Okuni's Kabuki Odori.

As the popularity of Young Men's Kabuki grew, the authorities were confronted with the same ethical problem that had been posed earlier by the Women's Kabuki, because the pretty boys and young men hired by Wakashu Kabuki troupes appealed to daimyo, samurai and well-to-do merchants with homosexual tendencies. The Tokugawa shogunate introduced strict measures to check the prevalence of such sexual behavior. Finally, in the summer of the first year of Jō'ō (1652), twenty-three years after the Women's Kabuki was banned, the staging of the Young Men's Kabuki was likewise prohibited.

One reason for the Tokugawa authorities to forbid performances by Wakashu Kabuki actors was to reinforce the earlier measures taken concerning Women's Kabuki troupes. Women had been banned from appearing on the stage because such performances became hotbeds of prostitution. Nonetheless, the authorities continued to have trouble with women trying to return to the field of entertainment. During the 1630s and 1640s, such popular young actors as Murayama Sakondayū, and Sakondayū's protégé, Ukon Genzaemon, went to Edo and began to present themselves in female roles wearing women's costumes. Taking advantage of that situation, some women attempted to appear on stage by mingling with the performers who were posing as women. By prohibiting the Young Men's Kabuki in 1652, therefore, the Tokugawa authorities hoped to finally put a stop to such attempts by women.

Measures to restrict the Women's Kabuki Odori or Young Men's Kabuki Odori were aimed generally at people belonging to the merchant class, but the authorities hoped also to intimidate daimyo and *hatamoto* (samurai serving the shogun) so that they would refrain from leading dissipated lifestyles, running up debts on courtesans or fighting with rival samurai over their amorous desires. But the state did not wish to eradicate Kabuki Odori entirely, and the townspeople in Edo and the Kyoto-Osaka region were allowed to continue going to theaters or pleasure quarters. By repeatedly issuing restrictive regulations, however, the authorities wanted to impress on people the idea that watching Kabuki Odori and seeking pleasure with professional women[9] were "morally bad" activities.

In accordance with shogunal decrees enforced in 1652, all the members of Young Men's Kabuki troupes, except just one very young actor in each troupe, had to change their hairstyle by shaving off the hair growing from the forepart of their heads — the symbol of the *wakashu*. During the period from 1653 to 1687, a striking change came about in the nature of Kabuki. From being Kabuki Odori, the genre became recognizable as simply Kabuki, a theatrical form — a change brought about by practitioners of the Young Men's Kabuki, now with their forelocks shaved in the *yarō* style.[10] Within a year of the Young Men's Kabuki being banned, Kabuki troupes managed to obtain permission from the authorities to stage performances on condition that the performers adopt the *yarō* hairstyle and that they offer only *monomane kyōgenzukushi* (plays that are all modeled on mimicry-based Kyōgen plays).[11]

The general trend across major genres of entertainment in Edo during the latter half of the 17th century is noted in the diary of Matsudaira Yamatonokami Naonori (1642-1695), a daimyo from the feudal domain of Murakami in Niigata Prefecture, who later became the lord of Himeji in Hyōgo Prefecture. Yamatonokami is known to have kept a diary for thirty-seven years from 1658 and his entries from 1659 to 1667[12] illustrate the young daimyo's avid interest in popular entertainment. Yamatonokami was stationed in Edo from the 11th day of the fourth month in the fourth year of Kambun (1664) to the 15th day of the fifth month of the following year, and his diary records thirty Nō and Kyōgen performances given at his residence or at those of other daimyo. Yamatonokami was so meticulous that he sent his retainers to different theaters and performances across Edo to see Kabuki and *ningyō jōruri*, and he recorded everything based on their reports.

In spite of the fact that public presentation of the Kabuki Odori was officially banned in 1652, the titles of various *odori* are found in Yamatonokami's diary. Popular dance numbers were often presented between the acts of *ningyō jōruri*. During the course of certain Kabuki plays classified as *monomane* plays,[13] untitled *odori* numbers were performed by young actors who wore the *wakashu* hairstyle, or by *onnagata* actors playing female roles.[14] The program of *monomane kyōgenzukushi* concluded ordinarily with a colorful dance performed by all the members of a Kabuki troupe, young and old.[15]

For three decades, until 1687, the eve of the Genroku Era, elements of the Kyōgen theater that had first been adopted by Okuni continued to be applied by actors with the *yarō* hairstyle to staging their Kabuki performances. As in the case of Okuni's performance, this Kabuki Odori included a Kyōgen-based skit complete with a scene of drinking, followed by *mai* dances performed by the principal actor and young *onnagata*, and a comical, rhythmic dance (*hyōshimai*) by the *dōke*. Adopting the realistic type of acting based on *monomane* unique to the Kyōgen theater, they produced Kabuki performances under the name of *monomane kyōgen*, which utilized the skill developed by the *dōke* of mimicking such people as an old woman or a *rōnin* (masterless samurai).

Among the Kabuki productions presented in Kyoto and Osaka during the 1650s and 1660s were a group of plays called Shimabara Kyōgen,[16] depicting scenes of men visiting the pleasure quarters of Shimabara in Kyoto. Almost half a century earlier, around 1617, licensed quarters had been established in the area of Rokujō at Misujimachi. In 1640, however, courtesans working in that area were moved to a location called Suzakuno, and this walled district came to be known as Shimabara since it was compared to the fortress of Shimabara in northern Kyūshū (famous for the suppression of Christians that had taken place there in 1638). The Shimabara Kyōgen, used as a preview of the area's female attractions for men intending to visit this district, may be considered a development of Okuni's Kabuki Odori, which also features realistic acting with comical touches. This step also led to the creation, during the 18th century, of Kabuki plays on the theme of *oie sōdō* (troubles in a daimyo's household) that invariably included scenes of men spending time in houses of pleasure.

While the Shimabara Kyōgen was banned several times during the 1650s and 1660s, there is evidence of plays called Keiseigoto no Kyōgen that were performed from 1661 to 1680, presenting ways to deal with courtesans. One such play, recorded in the *Geikagami* of late 17th-century date, begins with the grand entry of a *tachiyaku* in the role of a prospective client over the *hashigakari*. Fashionably dressed, the man carries a sword at his left hip; his left arm is bent at the elbow and he holds a folded fan in his right hand. The man announces that he has come to spend time with a courtesan, hitting the hilt of his sword with the fan. The proprietor of a pleasure house (*ageya*) appears from inside and welcomes the guest in a comical fashion. Anxious to gratify the man's eagerness to see the woman with whom he is to spend the evening, the proprietor announces that his courtesan can now be seen coming over the bridge. A splendidly costumed woman enters, and her appearance[17] certainly meets the expectations of the audience. She welcomes her client cordially by holding both his hands. The proprietor begins to serve sake to the guest, while urging the courtesan to dance for him. As requested, the courtesan performs a *mai* dance to the accompaniment of a drum and hand drums.

The Keiseigoto no Kyōgen depicted in the *Geikagami*, representing a wealthy man having a good time with a high-class courtesan, may also be considered a development of Okuni's Kabuki Odori. In this play, a *tachiyaku* performs the prospective client, a young *onnagata* enacts the courtesan, and a *dōke* employs comic touches to act the part of the proprietor of the house of pleasure. The basic Kabuki roles — *tachiyaku, onnagata, wakashugata,*[18] *katakiyaku*[19] and *dōke* — were established during the Empō Era (1673-1681), although records show variations in the way these roles were defined. The emergence of *katakiyaku* in the late Empō Era suggests that Kabuki had developed considerably as a dramatic form by that time, helped along by the creation of *tsuzuki kyōgen* (Kabuki plays having several acts) in the 1660s.[20]

Notes

1. There were a great many Nō performances by women in Kyoto from 1585 to around 1630, even after the theaters were relocated from the Kamo riverbed at Shijō.

2. The traditional form of *mai* dance performed to the recitation of epic texts, popular from the 14th to the 16th century.

3. The Kamo riverbed at Shijō began to flourish as an entertainment center after 1615, the year in which the Tokugawa forces won a decisive victory over those of Toyotomi in the siege of Osaka Castle.

4. Introduced from the Ryūkyū Islands in the Eiroku Era (1558-1570), the samisen was modified in Sakai before spreading throughout Japan.

5. A type of *kusemai* developed in the late Muromachi Period by a samurai named Momonoi Naonori, known in his youth as Kōwakamaru. Kōwakamai features the *Heike Monogatari* (Tales of the Taira Clan) and the stories of Minamoto no Yoshitsune and the Soga Brothers.

6. It is recorded in *Tokiyoshikyōki* on the 17th day of the ninth month in the eighth year of Keichō (1603) that a five-year-old boy performed Dōnan Kabuki Odori. Takei, Kyōzō. *Wakashu Kabuki · Yarō Kabuki no Kenkyū*, Tokyo · Yagi Shoten, 2000, p. 4.

7. Takei, *op. cit.*, p. 11.

8. The most notable among such actors were Saruwaka Kanzaburō and Ukon Genzaemon.

9. As early as 1617, certain women were allowed to be engaged in "business" in the licensed quarters of Moto Yoshiwara in Edo.

10. Sakata Takenojō with his hair done in the *yarō* style is illustrated in Kobayashi, Tadashi. *Edo no Bijinga*, Tokyo · Gakken, 1982, pl. 181. *Yarō* refers generally to young men with their forelocks shaved.

11. Takei, *op. cit.*, pp. 34-38.

12. Available in copies published in 1944. Takei, *op. cit.*, p. 85.

13. "*Kumasaka*," "*Byōbu Maotoko*" and "*Chanoyu Tanzen*," for example.

14. Gunji, Masakatsu. *Kabuki Ronsō*, Tokyo · Shibunkaku, 1979, p. 42.

15. Gunji, *ibid*.

16. So called because they were Kyōgen-based plays about Shimabara.

17. In those days, the *onnagata* taking the part of a courtesan usually had his hair tied in a knot called *hyōgo*, wrapped with a piece of paper.

18. *Wakashugata* is the generic role of a pretty young man with the *wakashu* hairstyle, but the term refers also to an actor who performs such a role.

19. *Kataki* means enemy; and *katakiyaku* is the villain or actor in that role.

20. Takei, *op. cit.*, p. 19. In case of *tsuzuki kyōgen*, the term *kyōgen* stands for Kabuki plays.

III   The Emergence of the *Onnagata*

The Genna Era (1615-1624), the period in which the Tokugawa regime consolidated its power after the destruction of Toyotomi Hideyori, saw young actors increasingly adopting the *wakashu* hairstyle and assuming a feminine demeanor. In fact, these young men looked just like women, and their model was Ariwara no Narihira, a renowned Heian nobleman of exceptional beauty. The *wakashu* actors, or *wakashugata,* were endowed with distinctly ungendered charm — if you thought that they were women, they were in fact men, and although you knew that they were men, they looked like women — and appealed to audiences of both sexes. During the 1630s and 1640s, when the Wakashu Kabuki, or Young Men's Kabuki, was in vogue, there emerged young actors who substituted for women in performing female characters. Those who specialized in female roles were now called *onnagata*, and such early *onnagata* as Murayama Sakondayū and Ukon Genzaemon were popular chiefly because of their good looks and enticing appearance, and on account of their skill in *odori* or *mai* dance. They were considered to appeal to men with homosexual tendencies, yet thanks to their femininity, they were also found attractive by heterosexual men (fig. 4).

The most prominent among the pioneer *onnagata* was Ukon Genzaemon[1] who was active in the second quarter of the 17th century. Born in 1622, Genzaemon went to Edo during the 1630s, apprenticed himself to Murayama Sakondayū who was active at the time, and enjoyed a reputation as the finest *onnagata* of the 1650s.[2] It is probable that Genzaemon received his initial stage training in Kyōgen, for his repertory included many numbers with Nō and Kyōgen origins. For instance, he is said to have performed, to the accompaniment of samisen music, a short *komai* dance called "*Nanatsu ni Naru Ko* (A Seven-year-old Boy)," holding an *uchiwa* (round fan).[3] With his Kyōgen background, Genzaemon presented *komai* dance — such as "*Nanatsu ni Naru Ko*," taken from a Kyōgen play — using stage props and instrumentation adopted by members of the Women's Kabuki Odori.

Wearing women's costume, Genzaemon, renowned for his beauty and his great skill in *mai* dance, captivated his audiences by presenting some Kyōgen plays in the Kabuki style. Among the paintings of beautiful women (*bijinga*) created in the Kambun Era (1661-1673), there are examples that are thought to depict Genzaemon.[4] Such early *onnagata* actors differed from the Kyōgen actors who performed female roles, since the latter merely imitated women's way of speaking and their gestures or movements.

Yoshizawa Ayame (1673-1729) was the first actor in the history of Kabuki who performed female characters of all kinds while being conscious of the fact that the *onnagata* is a man. Ayame established himself as a true *onnagata* by negating the notion of neutral beauty popularly held by the *onnagata* actors who had been active before him in the phase of Yarō Kabuki (Men's Kabuki) from 1653 to 1687. Before considering the career of this fascinating actor in greater detail, however, we must touch upon the Kabuki of the Genroku Era (1688-1704), a time characterized by a burst of artistic and cultural activity throughout Japan. From 1653 through the 1660s, Kabuki had begun to evolve as a dramatic system referred to as *tsuzuki kyōgen*. It first flowered in the Genroku Era, during which two strikingly different styles of Kabuki acting developed in Edo, the seat of the Tokugawa shogunate, and in Kyoto, the ancient capital of Japan. The two styles were spearheaded by Ichikawa Danjūrō I in Edo and by Sakata Tōjūrō in Kyoto, two *tachiyaku* of great talent and strikingly different temperaments.

Ichikawa Danjūrō I (1660-1704), an actor endowed with considerable charisma, started the Kabuki acting tradition referred to as *aragoto* in 1673 when he made his initial appearance as Danjūrō at the age of fourteen. The bombastic *aragoto* style, still practiced today, was highly appealing to Edo townspeople because it was evocative of the thrilling behavior of wild young warriors. The style was passed down the generations, and each Danjūrō, regarded as the "flower of Edo," sought to refine his acting technique in order to maintain the standards of the "art of the family" and to satisfy the expectations of

Edo townspeople. Danjūrō I is known to have written scripts for most of the plays he presented on the stage. In his productions, therefore, Danjūrō the actor and Danjūrō the playwright were powerfully fused.

Sakata Tōjūrō (1647-1709) in Kyoto first supervised the production of plays centering on the famous courtesan Yūgiri, who died in 1678 at the age of twenty-five. Tōjūrō's encounter in 1695 with Chikamatsu Monzaemon (1653-1724), the celebrated Bunraku and Kabuki playwright, enabled Tōjūrō to develop his gentle, sensuous acting style called *wagoto*. The actor was unrivaled in playing male leads in the *wagoto* style, and the 10-year collaboration of Sakata and Chikamatsu, beginning in 1695, produced many fascinating Kabuki plays, with plots often focusing on a daimyo in disguise or a wealthy merchant disowned as a result of his dissipated way of life. Such themes formed the mainstream of the Kabuki tradition in the *kamigata* region extending from Kyoto to Osaka.

Yoshizawa Ayame emerged in *kamigata* in the early 1690s. Acclaimed for his beauty and talent, Ayame was ranked *jō-jōkichi* (upper upper rank) as a young *onnagata* in 1698 for his outstanding performance of a courtesan named Miura in "*Keisei Asamagatake* (Courtesans Worshipping Mt. Asama)." Continuing to perform in the Kyoto-Osaka area, Ayame attained the prestigious status of *gokujō-jōkichi* (the uppermost rank) in 1711, a few years after the death of Sakata Tōjūrō. He turned up in Edo in 1713 and performed there for one year. After reaching the rank of *gokujō-jōkichi-murui* (the unprecedented, uppermost rank) in 1714, Ayame enjoyed the status of one of the foremost actors through the 1720s. In 1721, at the age of forty-seven, Ayame tried to change from being an *onnagata* to a *tachiyaku*, but within a year he resumed *onnagata* roles, which he continued for the rest of his life. Ayame had the reputation of being a better actor than dancer, and reigned over the early 18th-century Kabuki world as a performer unsurpassed in realistic acting. He was capable of expressing the innermost feelings of any female role, including the daughters and wives of samurai or merchants, but especially courtesans.

Late in life, Ayame wrote essays on the art of *onnagata* acting, which have survived under the title of *Ayamegusa* (Ayame's Sayings). *Ayamegusa* gives us an insight into Ayame's thoughts about his profession, his definition of the *onnagata* and the place of *onnagata* actors in the early 18th-century Kabuki theater. Moreover, the essays include valuable instructions to young men aspiring to become *onnagata* at the time. Ayame opens *Ayamegusa* by stating that if an *onnagata* is able to enact a *keisei* (high-ranking courtesan)[5] satisfactorily, he will find any other female role easy to handle. In his opinion, the courtesan should be beautiful, gentle and loving; a crystallization of the elements which men find most desirable in women. So Ayame maintains that it is essential for an *onnagata*, who is really a man, to transcend his own self in reaching toward the realization of a perfect courtesan, the ultimate embodiment of men's desires.

4.   Two groups of young performers — *onnagata* to the left and *wakashugata* to the right — share a stage to present Kabuki Odori (right-hand screen of pair of sixfold screens; datable to the late 1680s)

Courtesy of Idemitsu Bijutsukan, Tokyo

Ayame continues with remarks on the acting process. After grasping the individual nature of a particular character, a Kabuki actor, whether he be a *tachiyaku* or an *onnagata*, begins to tackle the task of building the character, depending on his skill and the style of acting he has mastered. His talent as an actor can only be given concrete form through his performances. Technique is the most powerful weapon the actor possesses to create an intense dramatic situation, and he should take pains to create the desired effect while performing. Nonetheless, Ayame adds, if an actor continues to seek acclaim by repeating the same performance, his art will become stagnant and uninteresting.

The most famous of all the courtesans who gave their names to the history of Kabuki is Yūgiri, a top-ranking *keisei* who first worked in the Shimabara district of Kyoto. For her extraordinary beauty and

pleasant temperament, her accomplishments in music and her exquisite way of lovemaking, Yūgiri was acclaimed as the "model of courtesans unprecedented in history" by Ihara Saikaku (1642-1693), the renowned author of *Kōshoku Ichidai Otoko* (Adventures of an Amorous Man). In the 12th year of Kambun (1672), Yūgiri moved to Osaka, when Ōgiya, the house of pleasure to which she belonged, transferred its location to Shinmachi. When she arrived in Osaka by boat on the Yodo River, the courtesan was welcomed by crowds of people anxious to see their idol. But five years later, she fell ill and died there in January of the sixth year of Empō (1678), at the age of twenty-five. Mourning over the early death of Yūgiri, Sakata Tōjūrō the following month dedicated to her a Kabuki play entitled "*Yūgiri Nagori no Shōgatsu* (The Last New Year's Day Celebrated by Yūgiri)." Yūgiri lives today as the splendid heroine of a well-known Kabuki play called "*Kuruwa Bunshō* (A Story of the Pleasure Quarters)," generally known as "*Yoshidaya*" (fig. 48), based on part of Chikamatsu Monzaemon's 1712 Bunraku masterpiece, "*Yūgiri Awa no Naruto* (Yūgiri at Naruto)."

Ayame had several sons, who followed in their father's footsteps by becoming Kabuki actors specializing in female roles. The oldest son succeeded to the stage name of Yoshizawa Ayame II on his father's death in 1729, and attained the rank of *gokujō-jōkichi* as an *onnagata* skilled at performing young women. Ayame's fourth son became Yoshizawa Ayame III in 1764, and also distinguished himself as a *gokujō-jōkichi onnagata*.

The most outstanding among Ayame's sons was his third son (1721-1786) who led a brilliant career in Edo as an *onnagata* with the stage name of Nakamura Tomijūrō, which he assumed in 1731. Handsome and gifted, Tomijūrō attained the pinnacle of Kabuki status by becoming *kabuki-ichidō-sōgeigashira* (head of all Kabuki actors) in 1785, one year before his death. While acclaimed for handling high-ranking courtesans and principal female characters in *jidaimono* (historical plays) and *sewamono* (realistic plays), Tomijūrō surpassed his father, Ayame, in the field of Kabuki dance, which was considered the specialty of the *onnagata* during the 18th century. The *onnagata* was not allowed to take the lead in any Kabuki play, and the dance was considered the only territory in which he could assert himself as the principal figure onstage and exhibit his accomplishment.

In the field of Kabuki dance, Tomijūrō competed with another prominent *onnagata* of the time having the stage name of Segawa Kikunojō (1693-1749), a performer who contributed to raising the standard of acting among the young *onnagata* of his time. Kikunojō retained so much of his youthful beauty at the age of sixty that he could wear the long-sleeved kimono ordinarily worn by unmarried young women. Kikunojō won acclaim in 1734 for creating such important dance numbers as "*Aioijishi*" and "*Makurajishi*," based on the famous Nō play "*Shakkyō*." Tomijūrō, on the other hand, enjoyed a great success with "*Musume Dōjōji*," which he presented in 1753, and with another version of the "*Shakkyō*" dance entitled "*Shūjakujishi*," staged the following year. Kabuki dance was only fully developed during the second and third quarters of the 18th century. Kikunojō and Tomijūrō created dances inspired by such famous Nō plays as "*Shakkyō*" and "*Dōjōji*," but these numbers were not direct "translations" of the Nō plays into dance. Instead the actors simply borrowed from them the essence, outlines and parts of the text. The Kabuki dance numbers based on "*Shakkyō*," "*Dōjōji*" and "*Sumidagawa* (The Sumida River)" are still very popular today.

By the end of the 18th century, the method of "character building" had been established by leading Kabuki actors specializing in female roles both in Edo and in the *kamigata* region. The efforts to improve the acting skill of the *onnagata*, which had been made by Yoshizawa Ayame and Segawa Kikunojō during the first half of the century, were continued by Segawa Kikunojō III, a gifted *onnagata* brought up in Osaka who had a reputation for his realistic style of acting. He went to Edo in 1773, at the age of twenty-five, and succeeded to the prestigious stage name of Segawa Kikunojō. Handsome and graceful, Kikunojō III remained extremely popular for several decades, being recognized as the finest *onnagata* of the 1780s and 1790s.[6]

According to the teaching and practice of Ayame and Kikunojō, the belief took hold that an *onnagata* should not merely imitate the speech, gesture and movement of the particular character he was enacting. To be a successful *onnagata*, the male actor must *become* a woman while performing on the stage. In addition to using elocution mastered through rigorous discipline and applying the technique of "character building" learned from his master or senior actors, the actor must grasp the inherent nature of the character. To render her true to life, he must perceive the character's individuality, giving consideration to such contextual matters as her status in society at the time when the play in question was written. The actor should stay with the innermost feelings of the character throughout his performance, whether the role be that of a courtesan or the daughter of a merchant.

Although created as a result of social changes in the 17th century, during which Kabuki Odori was banned twice, the *onnagata* soon became a unique and indispensable feature of the Kabuki theater.[7] The techniques of *onnagata* acting established by Ayame and Kikunojō continued to be practiced down the centuries, and Nakamura Jakuemon has long looked to Kikunojō as the model of the *onnagata*, regarding him as the source of inspiration for the pursuit of his vocation. Having performed innumerable *onnagata* roles over the past fifty years, adhering to the *kata* (acting patterns) he learned from Nakamura Utaemon VI, the most celebrated of 20th-century *onnagata*, Jakuemon has now reached the ultimate phase of his career. Each of his recent performances — whether as one of the famous *jidaimono* heroines, such as Yaegakihime, in the incense-burning scene from "*Honchō Nijūshikō* (The Twenty-four Models of Filial Piety: The Japanese Version)" or Sagami, wife of the gallant protagonist Kumagai Naozane in "*Kumagai Jin'ya* (Kumagai's Camp)" — demonstrates the quintessence of Jakuemon's *onnagata* art.

One important tenet left by the forerunners of the *onnagata* such as Ayame and Kikunojō is: To be a successful *onnagata*, an actor should become a woman while performing on the stage. With his long endeavors on the Kabuki stage, Jakuemon seems truly to have achieved this through his exquisitely contrived technique. Onstage, though,

Jakuemon gives the impression of being wholly "natural" in his performance. While enacting a particular role, Jakuemon is absolutely absorbed in it. But he has said that he feels as though Jakuemon the man is manipulating another Jakuemon, who is that woman, experiencing her joys or sorrows. Being manipulated by Jakuemon the man, the Jakuemon who is performing may feel at moments truly sad, or in some cases, totally deranged. Jakuemon has gone far beyond his Edo predecessors with this recognition of the *onnagata*'s two selves: One onstage performing, the other as it were behind the scenes, manipulating. And from time to time, the actor notes, he finds the two Jakuemons merge into one.

Notes

1. Takei, Kyōzō. *Wakashu Kabuki · Yarō Kabuki no Kenkyū*, Tokyo · Yagi Shoten, 2000, pp. 111-123.

2. Ukon Genzaemon is recorded as being thirty-seven years old in 1658.

3. Takei, *op. cit.*, pp. 14-15.

4. Kobayashi, Tadashi. *Edo no Bijinga*, Tokyo · Gakken, 1982, pl. 177.

5. At Shimabara in Kyoto, top-ranking courtesans were called *keisei* or *tayū*, followed by *tenjin*, *kakoi*, and *hanarejorō* at the bottom. Courtesans belonging to the *keisei* class were adored by men—daimyo, samurai and wealthy merchants alike. The general Japanese term for courtesans and prostitutes is *yūjo*.

6. Segawa Kikunojō III was portrayed in numerous ukiyo-e prints during the last quarter of the 18th century. His method of "character building" is discussed by Yukio Hattori in *Kabuki no Kōzō*, Chūkō Shinsho 237, Tokyo, 1970, p. 79 and pp. 92-93.

7. In staging a Kabuki play, a *jidaimono* in particular, the part of an *onnagata* cannot be replaced by an actress.

IV The Formation of Jakuemon's *Onnagata* Art

Nakamura Jakuemon is one of the rare Kabuki actors still acting today who served in the army during World War II. Anyone who sees him onstage now, an embodiment of femininity, would find it impossible to imagine him as a sergeant commanding a truck corps stationed in various locations in Southeast Asia.

The son of Kabuki actor Ōtani Tomoemon VI, Jakuemon made his debut as Hirotarō at the age of seven and soon gained a reputation as a Kabuki prodigy. To give his son proper training, Tomoemon had the young Hirotarō take lessons in the Gidayū music and narration used in Bunraku, Kabuki dance (under two different teachers), Nagauta and percussion music, acrobatics, and the tea ceremony.

Jakuemon was conscripted at the age of twenty, and when the war broke out, he was sent to the front. He miraculously survived six years of conflict, and at the war's end he was stationed on the island of Sumatra. By the time Jakuemon arrived home in late 1946, Kabuki had already been revived in the devastated city of Tokyo, where it was being performed at two venues — the Tōgeki (Tokyo Theater) and the Mitsukoshi Theater. As soon as he returned, Jakuemon went to Matsumoto Kōshirō VII, one of the leading Kabuki actors in Tokyo at the time, and expressed his desire to make a career as a Kabuki actor. Kōshirō suggested, to Jakuemon's great astonishment, that he become an *onnagata*. To set out at the age of twenty-seven, regarded as a "middle age" for Kabuki actors, on the rigorous path to becoming an *onnagata*, was an adventure in itself. Incredibly, the only alternative Jakuemon could think of was to become an automobile mechanic.

During the turbulent years of postwar Japan, everyone had to cling to something and struggle for a livelihood. Accepting Kōshirō's advice and backing, Jakuemon made becoming an *onnagata* his life's aim. For Jakuemon's coach, Kōshirō recommended the prominent *onnagata* Nakamura Utaemon VI, then called Shikan, who later became a dominant figure in the Kabuki theater. Jakuemon began by gaining experience of playing female roles on provincial tours. In

1947, though, he received recognition in Tokyo as a promising *onnagata* when he performed the part of Osono in a play titled "*Keyamura* (The Keya Village)" at the Mitsukoshi Theater. The following year, Jakuemon succeeded to the stage name of Ōtani Tomoemon VII, which he inherited from his father who had died during the war years. Jakuemon's marriage to the daughter of his mentor, Kōshirō, in the same year established his place in the Kabuki world. Not only was he now related by marriage to Kōshirō himself, but his brothers-in-law were Kōshirō's three actor-sons, namely, Ichikawa Danjūrō XI, Matsumoto Hakuō and Onoe Shōroku.

Life in postwar Japan was difficult for Kabuki actors. To support his growing family, in 1950 Jakuemon began to appear in films on historical subjects produced by the Tōhō Company movie studio. He became a star overnight with his initial appearance as the legendary early 17th-century swordsman Sasaki Kojirō, and from then on for several years he played the male lead in some thirty movies. Looking back upon his movie years, Jakuemon recalls feeling uncomfortable while being filmed because he had to follow the director's orders. Jakuemon prefers the Kabuki way of performing — each actor is his own master, drawing not on a director, but on the stores of acting patterns and theatrical conventions unique to his house.

In 1955, Jakuemon returned to the Kabuki stage in Tokyo, but was quickly sent to perform in Osaka. Kabuki was on the decline in Osaka, especially after the Kabukiza there was closed down in 1958. Luckily, Jakuemon found himself in the care of Ichikawa Jukai, the most eminent male lead, who allowed him to play important *onnagata* roles opposite him for nearly ten years. While he was coached personally by this great actor, Jakuemon enriched his repertory and prepared himself for his eventual return to Tokyo.

Back in Tokyo in 1964, the year of the Olympics, Jakuemon underwent at the Kabukiza the rite of succeeding to the stage name of Nakamura Jakuemon IV. The name would have been inherited by the son of Jakuemon III, Jakuemon's childhood friend, had he not been killed during the war. Of the two *onnagata* roles Jakuemon then performed, his Yukihime in "*Kinkakuji* (The Golden Pavilion)" was particularly significant. Chosen from the traditional repertory of the lineage of Nakamura Jakuemon, it was also the first Kabuki play Jakuemon saw on his return to Tokyo from his military service abroad. On the same occasion, Jakuemon's two sons succeeded to their respective stage names: The older son became Ōtani Tomoemon VIII, a *tachiyaku*, and the younger one, Nakamura Shibajaku VII, an *onnagata*.

What Jakuemon exhibits while performing on stage is extraordinarily beautiful, though highly contrived, which has been acquired by unstinting efforts over the years. When he is awake, he thinks of nothing but the stage, and this even stopped him from driving twenty years ago. (Jakuemon used to love to drive, trucks and motorcycles in particular.) Every movement he makes and every tone of voice he uses in delivering lines are carefully calculated. He is masterful in timing (*ma*) and in holding his breath before speaking his lines, skills acquired during his youthful training in Gidayū narration.

The quintessence of Jakuemon's art was seen in his presentation of Yukihime in "*Kinkakuji*" at the Kabukiza in March 1984. In its climactic scene, Jakuemon, dressed in an elegant pink kimono with long sleeves, is tied to a cherry tree with a piece of heavy rope. His body assumes a sensuously contorted posture as he tries to draw, using his right foot, a picture of a mouse in fallen cherry petals on the stage.

Jakuemon's acting is no less impressive in realistic *sewamono* plays written in the 19th century. An admirable example is his performance of Otomi, the mistress of a yakuza-like boss, in Segawa Jokō's 1853 masterpiece known as "*Genjidana*." Jakuemon learned the technique of acting in Kabuki plays of this type from an actor called Onoe Baichō, who was a disciple of Onoe Baikō VI and a veritable walking encyclopedia in Kabuki matters.

An *onnagata* thoroughly grounded in Kabuki classics, Jakuemon believes that each Kabuki actor should master the basic skills of his predecessors, but also holds that performances should appeal to contemporary audiences. The actor has high hopes for the creation of new Kabuki scripts in which *onnagata* can play significant parts.

Jakuemon is transformed when he is made up and in costume. He looks young and appealing on stage and makes his audience forget his real age. He is able to suggest youthfulness and freshness even when playing opposite handsome male leads who are considerably younger than he is. He is convinced that one of the keys to his youthful looks has been to take regular exercise over the years.

For Jakuemon, playing an *onnagata* part is the process of crystallizing femininity into restrained beauty. The *onnagata* also firmly believes that it is essential to relax once he is through with his work, to replenish his energy required for the next day's performance. The air tastes different, he says, when he enters the theater and his dressing room, and the actor appears able to switch himself on and off as required. For diversion, Jakuemon used to ride horses — as a child, he wanted to become a jockey or a cowboy. He says he enjoys riding because he feels strangely elevated while riding and he loves heights, saying that one day he would like to join Tokyo Tower's cleaning team.

Jakuemon is a fashionable dresser, but he confesses that most of the clothing with which he has surprised the public has been given to him by friends, some of whom are well-known designers. Once he started wearing such gifts, he explains, he found it great fun to dress boldly. Since the term "Kabuki" derives from the verb *kabuku* meaning "to be slanted" or "to wear exotic costume," Jakuemon, young at heart, seems to exemplify the true spirit of Kabuki by his dandyishness.

The actor is gentle, friendly and attentive. He has a dark complexion — a reminder, perhaps, of his long sojourn in Southeast Asia during the war years. The modern Kabuki stage has great reason to be thankful that Jakuemon returned home safely from his military duties, and that he was able to develop his talent as an *onnagata*.

(Featured in *The Japan Times* on June 21, 1986, titled,
"Jakuemon, the *onnagata* Kabuki actor.")

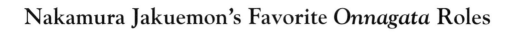

Nakamura Jakuemon's Favorite *Onnagata* Roles

Agemaki in "*Sukeroku*"

5.   Left to right: Ichikawa Danjūrō as Sukeroku, Nakamura Jakuemon as Agemaki and
the late Kawarazaki Gonjūrō as Ikyū in "*Sukeroku*"
(Kabukiza, May 1977)
Photograph by Yutaka Umemura

One of the eighteen famous Kabuki plays belonging to the Ichikawa line of
Kabuki actors, "*Sukeroku*" is very simple in plot but wonderfully enjoyable. Brisk
exchanges of witty, abusive remarks by Sukeroku, Agemaki, Ikyū and other
fascinating characters express the defiant spirit of 18th-century Edo townspeople.

Sukeroku, who is actually the legendary hero Soga no Gorō in disguise, makes his
grand entry along the *hanamichi* (flower-way stage passage) to the accompaniment of
lively Katōbushi music. Whenever Sukeroku enters the main gate to the Yoshiwara
pleasure quarters, he is showered with tobacco pipes by the courtesans as a sign of
their welcome. The reason Sukeroku frequents Yoshiwara — and picks a fight with
everyone he encounters there — is in the hope of finding a sword named
Tomokirimaru. He also visits Yoshiwara to see his courtesan-lover Agemaki, who is
being courted by Ikyū, a wealthy old man famous for his magnificent beard.
Suspecting Ikyū of having stolen the precious sword, Sukeroku tries to provoke the
old man into drawing his sword out of its sheath. When Sukeroku discovers that

Ikyū indeed carries the sword he has long been searching for, he wants to attack the old man on the spot, but is stopped by Agemaki with a commanding gesture.

Ever since it was created by Ichikawa Danjūrō II in 1713, "*Sukeroku*," which combines the bombastic *aragoto* acting tradition of Edo and some elements of the gentle *wagoto* style of acting unique to the Kyoto-Osaka region, has generally been performed by leading actors of the Ichikawa family. Shown on the facing page (fig. 5) is a marvelous photograph of Jakuemon playing Agemaki in May 1977, with the present Ichikawa Danjūrō (Jakuemon's nephew) as Sukeroku and the late Kawarazaki Gonjūrō as Ikyū. In two more recent photographs (below), showing the very last scene of the play, Jakuemon performs Agemaki opposite both Danjūrō (fig. 6) and Danjūrō's son, Shinnosuke (fig. 7), in the role of Sukeroku.

6. Ichikawa Danjūrō as Sukeroku (left) and Nakamura Jakuemon as Agemaki in the final scene of *"Sukeroku"* (Kabukiza, January 2003)
Photograph by Shōchiku Photographic Department

7. Ichikawa Shinnosuke as Sukeroku (left) and Nakamura Jakuemon as Agemaki in the final scene of *"Sukeroku"* (Shimbashi Embujō, January 2000)
Photograph by Shōchiku Photographic Department

Chiyo and Tonami in "*Terakoya* (Temple School)"

8. Nakamura Jakuemon as Tonami (left) and the late Ichimura Uzaemon XVII as Takebe Genzō
    in "*Terakoya*"
    (National Theater, December 1981)
    Photograph by Yutaka Umemura

"*Terakoya*" is a *jidaimono* masterpiece adapted from Act IV of the 1746 Bunraku play "*Sugawara Denju Tenarai Kagami* (Sugawara Certifies a Disowned Disciple to Perpetuate His Line of Calligraphy)" by Takeda Izumo and collaborators. "*Sugawara Denju Tenarai Kagami*" centers on the life of Sugawara Michizane, the renowned ninth-century scholar-politician, and his political rivalry with Fujiwara no Tokihira, Minister of the Left. The structure of the play is further complicated by the addition of stories about a celebrated set of triplets living in Osaka at the time the play was written. Of the three brothers, Umeōmaru serves Michizane; Sakuramaru is in the service of Prince Tokiyo, younger brother of the emperor; and Matsuōmaru works for Michizane's mortal enemy, Tokihira. "*Terakoya*" features the story of Matsuōmaru, who sacrifices his own son, Kotarō, in order to save the life of Michizane's young heir Kanshūsai, after Michizane has been exiled on charges of treason.

Matsuōmaru orders his wife, Chiyo, to take Kotarō to the *terakoya* (temple school) run by Takebe Genzō, Michizane's disowned disciple in calligraphy, intending Kotarō to be killed by Genzō in place of Kanshūsai, whom he is keeping in his custody. This indeed occurs, and the play climaxes as Matsuōmaru examines the severed head of his son and declares that it is the head of Kanshūsai. After Kotarō's head has been carried away by an officer, Chiyo returns and learns from Genzō that her son has been killed for Michizane's cause. She is joined by Matsuōmaru and, with Genzō and his wife Tonami, they mourn for the death of Kotarō, to the melancholy tune of Gidayū music.

Jakuemon is photographed first as Tonami (fig. 8) introducing Kotarō to her husband Genzō (performed by the late Ichimura Uzaemon XVII), who has come home troubled with the need to find a substitute boy who can be sacrificed in place of Michizane's son. The photograph below (fig. 9) shows Jakuemon as Chiyo who, having just returned to Genzō's house, is trying to find out what has happened there during her absence.

9. Nakamura Jakuemon as Chiyo in *"Terakoya"*
(Kabukiza, March 2000)
Photograph by Fumio Watanabe

Hanako in "*Musume Dōjōji* (The Maiden of Dōjōji Temple)"

10. Nakamura Jakuemon as Hanako striking the final pose of
     "*Musume Dōjōji*"
     (Kabukiza, April 1991)
     Photograph by Shōchiku Photographic Department

An extraordinary hour-long dance created by Nakamura Tomijūrō I in 1753, modeled after the famous Nō play "*Dōjōji*," "*Musume Dōjōji*" is performed on a striking stage with an enormous temple bell hanging against a backdrop of cherry blossoms, to the accompaniment of dazzling Nagauta music played by an impressive array of onstage musicians. "*Musume Dōjōji*" is one of the most important dance numbers for *onnagata* actors because it demands all the essential techniques of Kabuki dance required by the *onnagata*.

In the first of these photographs (fig. 11), Jakuemon appears on the *hanamichi* as the enchanting priestess Hanako, who has traveled to Dōjōji Temple in Wakayama Prefecture hoping to see a bronze bell which has been newly dedicated to the temple. The lovely priestess, however, is actually the spirit of the legendary heroine Kiyohime in disguise. Infatuated with a handsome Buddhist monk, Anchin, Kiyohime once transformed herself into a giant snake in order to chase him to Dōjōji. There she killed him by trapping him in the temple bell and then coiling herself around it — the tremendous heat generated by her body burned alive the unfortunate Anchin. As Hanako she now revisits the temple, where, requested by a group of acolytes working there, she begins to dance under the cherry trees. After taking off her ceremonial golden hat, she is revealed as a winsome *musume* (maiden) and in her dance portrays various aspects of her experiences in love, occasionally displaying her attachment to the bell. The dance climaxes as the young woman displays her true, serpentine nature by exposing a white kimono decorated with a pattern of silver scales.

Although *"Musume Dōjōji"* was modeled after a Nō play, its connection with that original is seen only at the beginning and the end of the dance. The main body of the work consists of a set of dances popular at the time that depict young women's experiences in love, the highlight being the passage known as "Lessons in Love" (fig. 12). *"Musume Dōjōji"* is a fascinating dance to watch, as the performer changes his costume onstage several times, a technique known as *hikinuki*.

The series of five photographs shown here illustrate Jakuemon's performance of *"Musume Dōjōji,"* from the Nō-based introduction (fig. 11) to the final passage (fig. 10) in which Hanako climbs on top of the enormous bell (which has fallen to the ground) and strikes an imposing *mie* pose on top of the bell, signifying her serpentine identity.

11. Nakamura Jakuemon as Hanako
     arriving at the gate to Dōjōji
     Temple in *"Musume Dōjōji"*
     (Kabukiza, April 1996)
     Photograph by Akira Iwata

12. Nakamura Jakuemon as Hanako
     dancing "Lessons in Love" from
     "Musume Dōjōji"
     (Kabukiza, April 1996)
     Photograph by Akira Iwata

14. Nakamura Jakuemon as Hanako dancing with *suzudaiko* (hand drums with bells) in *"Musume Dōjōji"* (Kabukiza, April 1996)

Photograph by Akira Iwata

13. Nakamura Jakuemon as Hanako performing "The Famous Mountains" from *"Musume Dōjōji"* (Kabukiza, April 1996)

Photograph by Akira Iwata

Hanjo in "*Sumidagawa* (The Sumida River)"

15. Nakamura Tomijūrō as the ferryman (left) and Nakamura Jakuemon as Hanjo in "*Sumidagawa*" (Kabukiza, March 2000)
Photograph by Shōchiku Photographic Department

Created by Ichikawa Ennosuke's grandfather En'ō in 1919, using a piece of Kiyomoto music composed by Enjudayū IV, this dance drama is based on the famous Nō play "*Sumidagawa*," Kanze Motomasa's early 15th-century version of the medieval legend of Umewakamaru. This young boy was the son of a nobleman in Kyoto who, after being kidnapped, fell ill by the Sumida River in Edo and there died. "*Sumidagawa*" was one of Nakamura Utaemon's favorite dance pieces. He performed it frequently for forty years after his debut as Umewakamaru's mother, Hanjo, in 1953. Jakuemon performed Hanjo for the first time in April 1997 under the late Utaemon's tutelage, and the photographs shown here were taken during his performance in March 2000.

One spring day, late in the afternoon, Hanjo arrives at the Sumida River. She is exhausted, as she has traveled all the way from Kyoto looking for her abducted son, Umewakamaru. While roaming by the river, she meets a kind ferryman and hears from him the sad story of a twelve-year-old boy who died by the river exactly a year ago (fig. 15). When Hanjo learns the name of the hapless child, she bursts out sobbing, in grief. Led to the spot where the boy is buried, marked by a young weeping willow, Hanjo hears the voice of her son reciting the name of the Buddha Amitābha. She sees the phantom of Umewakamaru and darts about after it (fig. 16), finally falling to the ground and embracing the small burial mound (fig. 17), imagining that she is hugging her son, now lost forever.

In "*Sumidagawa*," the performer is expected to express Hanjo's sorrow in highly controlled movements. Jakuemon succeeds in conveying her despair, too, through subtle facial expressions and the exquisite use of his body and hands. Jakuemon's performance is enhanced by the skillful rendition of the sympathetic ferryman by Nakamura Tomijūrō, Jakuemon's partner in Kabuki dance for several decades.

16. Nakamura Tomijūrō as the ferryman (behind) and Nakamura Jakuemon as Hanjo in "*Sumidagawa*" (Kabukiza, March 2000)

Photograph by Shōchiku Photographic Department

17. Nakamura Jakuemon as Hanjo embracing the tomb of her son, Umewakamaru, in "*Sumidagawa*" (Kabukiza, March 2000)

Photograph by Shōchiku Photographic Department

Izayoi in "*Izayoi Seishin* (Izayoi and Seishin)"

18.   Nakamura Jakuemon as Izayoi (left) and Onoe Kikugorō as Seishin
       in "*Izayoi Seishin*" (Kabukiza, May 1979)
       Photograph by Yutaka Umemura

"*Izayoi Seishin*" is part of Kawatake Mokuami's 1859 *sewamono* masterpiece recounting the decadent love of the courtesan Izayoi and a young Buddhist acolyte called Seishin. Here, Jakuemon plays Izayoi in the style of acting he learned from Onoe Baichō, a disciple of Onoe Baikō VI, alongside Kikugorō Onoe, the finest actor of the role of Seishin today. In the first scene, performed to the accompaniment of melancholic Kiyomoto music, Izayoi appears onstage having fled from the pleasure quarters in Ōiso. She has run away after hearing of Seishin's expulsion from Gokurakuji Temple in Kamakura because of his amorous involvement with her. On the bank of the Inase River, Izayoi encounters her lover, who is on his way to Kyoto where he intends to resume his course of spiritual discipline as a Buddhist monk. Unable either to leave Izayoi or take her to Kyoto with him, Seishin agrees to die with her, and the two resolve to commit suicide by throwing themselves into the river.

Izayoi, however, is saved from drowning by Hakuren, a notorious burglar disguised as a Haiku poet, who has been fishing in the night. Meanwhile, Seishin, a strong swimmer, is having trouble drowning himself downstream. When he tries to jump into the river for the second time, a pretty boy (Izayoi's younger brother, whom Seishin has never met) approaches, and then collapses with acute chest pains. While nursing the boy, Seishin discovers that he is carrying a package of 50 *ryō*. He entreats the boy to lend him the money, but is fiercely refused. Trying to wrestle the wallet away from the boy, Seishin accidentally chokes him with the cord tied to it. After this inadvertent murder, Seishin thinks of killing himself using the boy's sword, but as the moon looms through the dark clouds, he changes his mind and dumps the dead body into the river. The sound of the body hitting the water ironically reaches Izayoi, who happens to be passing by in the company of Hakuren, who holds an umbrella over her. Seishin hurries away, secretly pleased with the weight of the 50 *ryō* in his hand.

Kasane in "*Kasane*"

19.   Nakamura Jakuemon as Kasane in "*Kasane*" (Kabukiza, April 1999)
       Photograph by Yutaka Umemura

A dance drama which is grotesque yet beautiful, "*Kasane*" is part of a Kabuki play (with an all-but-untranslatable title), "*Kesakakematsu Narita no Riken*," written by Tsuruya Namboku IV and presented in Edo in 1823.

Kasane is desperately in love with Yoemon, a handsome farmer with a samurai background, who unbeknownst to her had once seduced Kasane's mother and killed her father. Yoemon has fled Edo after having an affair with Kasane, but Kasane pursues him, concealing her face with a purple silk scarf. Catching up with Yoemon on the bank of the Kine River, Kasane tells him that she is three months pregnant, and begs him to die with her (fig. 19). When Yoemon finally yields to her entreaties, he finds a human skull floating down the stream on a wooden votive tablet with a rusty sickle stuck into its left eye socket! Recognizing the skull as that of Kasane's father, whom he had murdered, Yoemon breaks the tablet in two. Instantly, Kasane falls to the ground and becomes crippled. And as Yoemon pulls the sickle out of the skull, the left side of Kasane's lovely face is suddenly disfigured — the effect of a curse laid on her by the dead man. Even more frightening is a sudden change that takes place in Yoemon. He strikes Kasane with the sickle (fig. 20), and ruthlessly forces her to look at her horrible face in a hand mirror by moonlight. After killing Kasane with a fatal blow, Yoemon tries to flee — but in vain. By the mysterious motions of her left hand, Kasane's ghostly figure draws back Yoemon to where she stands (fig. 21).

The photographs here show Jakuemon as Kasane and Nakamura Kichiemon as Yoemon, taken during their performance at the Kabukiza in April 1999. They performed according to the style of staging "*Kasane*" established by Onoe Baikō VI and Ichimura Uzaemon XV in 1920.

20. Nakamura Kichiemon as Yoemon (left) and Nakamura Jakuemon as Kasane in "*Kasane*" (Kabukiza, April 1999)
Photograph by Akira Iwata

21. Nakamura Jakuemon as Kasane in the final scene of "*Kasane*" (Kabukiza, April 1999)
Photograph by Akira Iwata

Matsuyama in "*Ninin Wankyū* (Wankyū in a Dream)"

22. Nakamura Jakuemon as the phantom of Matsuyama in *"Ninin Wankyū"* (Kabukiza, September 2000)
Photograph by Fumio Watanabe

"*Ninin Wankyū*" is a highlight of classical Kabuki dance based on the story of Wan'ya Kyūbei, a wealthy merchant in Osaka who died insane in 1677 after spending all his fortune on Matsuyama, the most famous courtesan in the Shinmachi pleasure district. The story of Wan'ya Kyūbei — abbreviated to Wankyū — became so widely known in Osaka that it was taken up in Kabuki and Bunraku dramas during the 18th century. The scene in which Wankyū wanders after the phantom of his beloved Matsuyama was considered an ideal subject for a dance number, and "*Ninin Wankyū*" was choreographed by the noted dance master Onoe Kikunojō I in the 1950s to be performed to the accompaniment of Nagauta music.

Wearing a sheer black jacket and a purple cap, and carrying a cane, which suggests his deranged state of mind, Wankyū enters down the *hanamichi* and roams about the stage beneath an enormous pine tree and a huge half-moon that hangs in

23.　Nakamura Jakuemon as Matsuyama (left) and Nakamura Tomijūrō as Wankyū in *"Ninin Wankyū"* (Kabukiza, September 2000)

Photograph by
Shōchiku Photographic Department

the dark sky. He falls asleep under the pine tree, and there appears to him in his dream Matsuyama (fig. 22), splendidly dressed in a trailing white robe decorated with a *matsu* (pine tree) symbolizing her name. Recollecting the happy times they spent together, Wankyū and Matsuyama dance joyously (fig. 23). Eventually, though, Matsuyama's apparition disappears, leaving Wankyū alone and in a state of collapse.

Ever since their initial performance of *"Ninin Wankyū"* in 1956, Jakuemon has danced Matsuyama exclusively with Nakamura Tomijūrō as Wankyū. *"Ninin Wankyū"* is eternalized by their brilliant performances, as illustrated in these photographs, taken in September 2000.

Omiwa in "*Imoseyama Onna Teikin*
(Admonitions to Women on Their Relationship With Men)"

24.   Left to right: Nakamura Shikan as Tachibanahime, Nakamura Jakuemon as Omiwa and
Onoe Kikugorō as Motome in the *michiyuki* scene of "*Imoseyama Onna Teikin*"
(Kabukiza, May 1988)   Photograph by Yutaka Umemura

"*Imoseyama Onna Teikin*" is an exciting *jidaimono* adapted from the five-act Bunraku play with the same title written by Chikamatsu Hanji and collaborators in 1771. It centers on the atrocious deeds of the seventh-century strongman, Soga no Iruka, who schemes to usurp the throne, and tells of his overthrow by Emperor Tenji and Minister Fujiwara no Kamatari in the Taika coup d'état of A.D. 645. "*Imoseyama Onna Teikin*" incorporates certain legends originating in the ancient Yamato region which extended from Nara to Osaka. The story of Omiwa, the tragic heroine of Act IV, is taken from one such local legend. In order to understand the meaning of Omiwa's death at the end of the play, we need to recall the folk belief that Iruka would lose his superhuman power upon hearing the sound of a flute that had been smeared with the blood of a black-hoofed deer and a young woman killed in a fit of jealousy.

Omiwa is the lovely, impetuous daughter of a wine producer in Yamato Province who is deeply in love with her handsome neighbor, Motome. He, however,

68

25. Nakamura Jakuemon as
Omiwa in the final scene of
"*Imoseyama Onna Teikin*"
(Kabukiza, November 1998)
Photograph by Fumio Watanabe

is actually Minister Kamatari's son Tankai, and is bent on destroying the archenemy Iruka. After fighting over Motome in front of a small local shrine with a pretty young woman, who turns out to be Iruka's younger sister, Tachibanahime (fig. 24), Omiwa chases Motome as he wanders away after her rival. Omiwa then strays into Iruka's sumptuous residence at the foot of Mikasayama (fig. 25), where she learns that Motome is about to marry Tachibanahime. (Motome has promised Tachibanahime that he will marry her if she retrieves his precious sword from Iruka.) As Omiwa is tormented by a group of vicious ladies-in-waiting, her expression changes and as a sign of her agitation she exposes her right shoulder, covered with a bright red undergarment. Now frantic with jealousy, Omiwa is about to run into the palace when she is stabbed by Kamatari's retainer, Kanawa no Gorō, disguised as a fisherman. Omiwa feels appeased and dies peacefully, however, when she hears from Gorō that she has been sacrificed because her blood is needed by her beloved Motome to destroy Iruka.

Jakuemon performs Omiwa in the style of acting he learned upon his succession to his stage name in 1964 from the late Nakamura Utaemon, whose performances of Omiwa are still regarded as unsurpassed.

Onoe in "*Kagamiyama Kokyō no Nishiki-e* (Scenes of the Daimyō's Household at Kagamiyama)"

26.   Nakamura Jakuemon as Onoe in
"*Kagamiyama Kokyō no Nishiki-e*"
(Kabukiza, June 1990)

Photograph by Yutaka Umemura

The stylized and beautiful "*Kagamiyama Kokyō no Nishiki-e*" is an excellent *jidaimono*, adapted from an eleven-act Bunraku play written by a physician with the pen name of Yō Yōtai and first performed in Edo in 1782. Belonging to a group of Bunraku and Kabuki plays on the theme of troubles in the house of Daimyo Maeda, the lord of the domain of Kaga in southern Ishikawa Prefecture, Yō Yōtai's "*Kagamiyama*" centers on a wicked scheme to usurp a provincial daimyo. The drama proved extremely popular among the Edo townsfolk because it was based on an actual incident that took place in the city in 1724, at the residence of Daimyo Matsudaira from Hamada in western Shimane Prefecture. Out of the lengthy, complicated Bunraku play, Acts VI and VII, featuring the conflict of three remarkable women — Iwafuji, Onoe and Ohatsu — have survived.

In "*Kagamiyama*," the chief lady-in-waiting, Iwafuji, who plots with the chief

27. Nakamura Jakuemon as Onoe just after being struck by Iwafuji in "*Kagamiyama Kokyō no Nishiki-e*" (Kabukiza, September 1994)

Photograph by Akira Iwata

retainer against the house of the daimyo she serves, is played not by an *onnagata* but by a *tachiyaku* (male lead). A splendid villain, Iwafuji is jealous of her rival Onoe, the second-rank lady-in-waiting, because the latter is favored by the daimyo's daughter and has been entrusted with a block of incense and an image of Amida (Amitābha) Buddha treasured by the family.

Jakuemon is superb as Onoe, who is a model of patience, enduring slights provoked by her lowly origins in the merchant class. She withstands Iwafuji's insults until one day she is accused by her of placing Iwafuji's slipper in the box that is supposed to contain the valuable incense to be presented to the shogun's messenger. Iwafuji viciously strikes the meek Onoe with the slipper. After this public humiliation, Onoe collects herself and begins to walk home (fig. 26), accompanied by a rueful tune of Gidayū music. Torn inside but outwardly keeping her composure, Onoe walks along the *hanamichi* passageway, contemplating suicide.

Onoe indeed takes her own life, but her death is avenged by her faithful maid, Ohatsu, the bright young daughter of an impoverished samurai, whose devotion to Onoe is very touching. After taking revenge on Iwafuji, Ohatsu is handsomely rewarded — she is promoted to the position held formerly by her beloved mistress.

Otatsu in "*Natsumatsuri Naniwa Kagami* (The Summer Festival in Osaka)"

28. Nakamura Jakuemon as Otatsu (left) and Nakamura Tomijūrō as Sabu in "*Natsumatsuri Naniwa Kagami*" (Kabukiza, September 1993) Photograph by Yutaka Umemura

Adapted from the 1745 Bunraku play by Namiki Senryū, Miyoshi Shōraku and Takeda Koizumo, the three-act "*Natsumatsuri Naniwa Kagami*," rendered in the Osaka dialect, centers on an exciting character named Danshichi Kurobei, who makes a modest livelihood by selling fish. Though among the lower social echelons of Osaka (at that time known as Naniwa), Danshichi belongs to the type of men referred to as *otokodate*, admired by the 18th-century Japanese for their keen sense of loyalty and chivalrous spirit. The drama revolves around Danshichi's loyalty to his former samurai master, Tamashima Hyōdayū, his friendship with Sabu and Tokubei, and his fatal relationship with his vicious father-in-law Giheiji. Danshichi's determination to help Hyōdayū's disowned son, Isonojō, brings trouble to his family and friends. When Isonojō's courtesan-lover, Kotoura, is abducted by Giheiji, Danshichi pursues Giheiji and kills him while trying to rescue Kotoura.

"*Natsumatsuri*" begins with a scene in which Danshichi, just released from jail,

29. Nakamura Jakuemon as Otatsu in *"Natsumatsuri Naniwa Kagami"* (Kabukiza, June 1999)

Photograph by Fumio Watanabe

is reunited with his old friend Sabu in front of the Sumiyoshi Shrine in Osaka. At the shrine Danshichi has a run-in with a hot-blooded man named Issun Tokubei, but after a scuffle, the two overcome their differences and pledge brotherhood. The following scene at Sabu's house focuses on Tokubei's remarkable wife Otatsu, who is strong enough to disfigure her lovely face with a horrible burn in order to convince Sabu to let her take Isonojō into her custody. She leaves with Isonojō, proudly declaring that her husband loves her not for her face but for her heart. In September 1993 and in June 1999, Jakuemon gave outstanding performances as Otatsu (figs. 28 and 29) in the style of acting he had learned from the late Nakamura Kanzaburō in 1968. On both occasions he performed opposite Nakamura Tomijūrō in the part of old Sabu.

"Natsumatsuri" ends with a showdown between Danshichi and his malicious father-in-law, in a scene titled "Behind Nagamachi Street." Enraged by Giheiji's persistent taunting, Danshichi chases Giheiji until he kills the wretched old man. Stripping himself to expose his magnificently tattooed back and limbs, Danshichi strikes *mie* poses while stabbing Giheiji, who is drenched with mud, to the lively sound of festive drums in the background.

Otoku in "*Domomata* (Matahei Who Stammers)"

30.   Nakamura Kichiemon as Matahei (left) and Nakamura Jakuemon as Otoku in "*Domomata*"
(Kabukiza, September 1991)   Photograph by Shōchiku Photographic Department

"*Domomata*" is a charming play adapted from part of "*Keisei Hangonkō*" (A Courtesan Burning Incense to See Visions of the Departed)," a historical Bunraku play written by Chikamatsu Monzaemon in 1708. It centers on Matahei, an honest, serious-minded man determined to become a certified painter of the Tosa School in spite of his speech impediment. Accompanied by his wife, Otoku, Matahei arrives in Yamashina, outside Kyoto, to visit his renowned master in exile, Tosa Mitsunobu. Envious of Mitsunobu's young disciple Shurinosuke, who has been given a diploma, Matahei, with the help of his vivacious wife, entreats Mitsunobu to grant him a diploma also. Rejected by his master, the despairing Matahei tries to stab himself. However, Otoku intervenes. Before he takes his own life, she suggests, he should leave his portrait on one side of a stone basin standing near the veranda of his master's house. After gazing at the reflection of his face in the water, Matahei paints his self-portrait on the back of the basin. He then prepares to complete his suicide, only to be stopped by Otoku, who tells him that the *sumi* ink lines of his painting

74

have penetrated the stone and emerged on the other side of the basin. Impressed by the power of Matahei's brushwork, the old master decides instantly to certify him as a full-fledged painter, bestowing upon him the name of Tosa Mitsuoki.

One of the most accomplished of living *onnagata* actors in the enactment of Matahei's devoted wife, Otoku, Jakuemon is shown in a photograph taken in November 1978 (fig. 31), urging Matahei (performed by the late Jitsukawa Enjaku) to paint his portrait on the basin before killing himself. In the photograph on the facing page, taken in September 1991 (fig. 30), Jakuemon plays opposite his nephew Nakamura Kichiemon. Here, Jakuemon's performance as Otoku is particularly expressive when she implores him, after finishing his portrait, to wait a little longer before killing himself.

31. Nakamura Jakuemon as Otoku (left) and the late Jitsukawa Enjaku III as Matahei in "*Domomata*" (Kabukiza, November 1978)

Photograph by Yutaka Umemura

Otomi in "*Genjidana*"

32.　　Nakamura Jakuemon as Otomi at the moment of
　　　recognizing her lover, Yosaburō, in "*Genjidana*"
　　　(Imperial Theater, December 1974)
　　　Photograph by Yutaka Umemura

　　　The one-act play known as "*Genjidana*" is part of Segawa Jokō's 1853 *sewamono* masterwork, "*Yowa Nasake Ukina no Yokogushi* (The Passions of a Woman With a Comb in Her Hair)." This tells of the love of Yosaburō, a young ruffian who makes a living by extortion, and Otomi, the attractive mistress of a yakuza. The scene is set three years after their initial encounter by the shores of Kisarazu in Chiba Prefecture. Yosaburō was a naive playboy when he first met Otomi, and he fell in love with her at first sight. However, he has changed drastically in the intervening years when he re-encounters Otomi in her house in Kamakura, where she now lives with a middle-aged man named Tazaemon (who turns out to be her older brother). The transformation of Yosaburō from a handsome young playboy to a yakuza-like extortionist revealed in this scene is the most exciting moment of the play. Yosaburō looks dangerous yet irresistible, with numerous scars on his face inflicted by Otomi's former yakuza patron three years previously when he discovered their illicit love affair.

Jakuemon's Otomi is shown below (fig. 33) returning home from a nearby public bathhouse. In the facing photograph (fig. 32), she is caught in the very moment of recognizing one of her uninvited visitors as Yosaburō, and her face and posture betray the essentially sensuous and decadent nature of her character. Jakuemon is indebted to Onoe Baichō, a disciple of Onoe Baikō VI and a walking encyclopedia of Kabuki lore, for teaching him how to portray fascinating *sewamono* characters such as Otomi.

33. Nakamura Jakuemon as Otomi returning from the bathhouse in "*Genjidana*" (Imperial Theater, December 1974)

Photograph by Yutaka Umemura

Sagami in "*Kumagai Jin'ya* (Kumagai's Camp)"

34.   Nakamura Jakuemon as Sagami lamenting over the severed head
of Kojirō in *"Kumagai Jin'ya"*
(Kabukiza, October 1987)
Photograph by Yutaka Umemura

"*Kumagai Jin'ya*" is a splendid *jidaimono* adapted from Act III of "*Ichinotani Futaba Gunki* (Records of the Battle at Ichinotani)," a Bunraku play written by Namiki Senryū and others in 1751 recounting the famous battle fought between the Minamoto and Taira forces in 1184. The play focuses on Kumagai Naozane, a martial hero affiliated with the victorious Minamoto clan, who has killed his sixteen-year-old son Kojirō to save the life of Prince Atsumori, the son of the retired emperor Goshirakawa. He acted in accordance with Minamoto no Yoshitsune's secret instructions, written on a wooden placard standing beside a cherry tree blooming in the soldiers' camp.

When Kumagai opens the lid of the wooden casket containing a severed head for Yoshitsune to examine its contents, Kumagai's wife Sagami is shocked to see her son's head—whereas Lady Fuji (Goshirakawa's consort) is astounded at not seeing the head of her son Atsumori. Kumagai strikes an imposing *mie* pose as he prevents the two women from rushing toward the head by holding, upside down, the wooden placard bearing Yoshitsune's instructions. The head of Kojirō is deemed by Yoshitsune to be that of Atsumori. The young prince, who is alive and hidden in a lacquered armor chest, is then entrusted to the stonemason Midaroku, who had once saved the lives of Yoshitsune and his mother Tokiwa. Kumagai reappears at the close of the scene in the guise of a Buddhist mendicant. He takes leave of Yoshitsune and sets out on a journey toward the Western Paradise of the Buddha Amitābha, praying for his son whom he has killed for the cause.

The style of acting the gallant protagonist, Kumagai, was perfected by Ichikawa Danjūrō IX, one of the most prominent Kabuki actors of the 19th-century. Danjūrō's style was handed down to Nakamura Kichiemon I and Matsumoto Kōshirō VII, then to Kōshirō's sons (Ichikawa Danjūrō XI, Matsumoto Hakuō and Onoe Shōroku) and grandsons (Ichikawa Danjūrō XII, Matsumoto Kōshirō IX and Nakamura Kichiemon II). Jakuemon played Sagami for the first time in 1964, opposite his brother-in-law Danjūrō XI as Kumagai. In the past fifteen years, he has often performed Sagami opposite his nephews Nakamura Kichiemon and Matsumoto Kōshirō.

Taemahime in "*Narukami*"

35.   Nakamura Kichiemon as Narukami (left) and Nakamura Jakuemon as Taemahime in "*Narukami*" (Kabukiza, January 1993)   Photograph by Yutaka Umemura

Part of "*Narukami Fudō Kitayamazakura* (Narukami's Soul Delivered by the Fudō at Kitayama)," initially presented by Ichikawa Danjūrō II in 1742, "*Narukami*" has been one of Kabuki's most popular plays ever since it was revived by Ichikawa Sadanji II in 1910, using a script written by the renowned Kabuki critic Oka Onitarō. The play is based on the legend of a holy man named Ikkaku from the Nō play "*Ikkaku Sennin.*" Ikkaku loses his supernatural power after peeping at a young woman's legs while she washes clothes in a river. In the Kabuki play, Ikkaku is known as Narukami. "*Narukami*" focuses on the exquisite way in which a woman named Kumo no Taemahime seduces the austere Buddhist monk, leading to his eventual downfall.

Taemahime has been sent to Kitayama, north of Kyoto, by the imperial court. She is entrusted with a mission to rob Narukami of his mysterious powers, because he has caused a severe drought across the country by confining the king of the dragons in the great waterfall behind his cottage. The theme of a powerful but naive man being destroyed by his carnal desires is a universal one, and the play ends with Narukami's realization that he has been betrayed by the woman to whose charms he has succumbed. Narukami's fierce explosion of wrath is conveyed by the traditional *aragoto* style of Kabuki acting (fig. 37), in a thunderstorm generated by Taemahime's release of the dragon king from the waterfall.

In the two photographs taken in August 1986 and January 1993, Jakuemon as Taemahime is shown in the process of seducing Narukami, performed by Ichikawa Danjūrō (fig. 36) and Nakamura Kichiemon (fig. 35), both of whom are his nephews. Jakuemon's Taemahime is consummately feminine, mature and enticing.

36. Ichikawa Danjūrō as Narukami (left) and Nakamura Jakuemon as Taemahime in *"Narukami"*
(Affiliated Public Cultural Hall, August 1986)
Photograph by Yutaka Umemura

37. Nakamura Kichiemon as Narukami consumed by a frenzy of wrath in *"Narukami"* (Asakusa Public Hall, January 1980)
Photograph by Yutaka Umemura

Takiyasha in "*Masakado*"

38. Ichikawa Danjūrō as Ōya Mitsukuni (left) and Nakamura Jakuemon as Takiyasha
accompanied by her familiar, the toad, in the final scene of "*Masakado*"
(National Theater, January 1992)   Photograph by Akira Iwata

Takiyasha, the heroine of the striking dance drama "*Masakado*" created in 1836, has been one of Jakuemon's favorite roles ever since he first performed it at the Misonoza Theater in Nagoya in 1976. For that initial performance Jakuemon was coached by Fujima Fujiko, the eminent teacher of Kabuki dance who had studied under Jakuemon's father-in-law, Matsumoto Kōshirō VII. Shown on the cover of this volume is a stunning shot of Jakuemon as Takiyasha, a splendidly attired courtesan holding an umbrella, as she makes her entrance down the *hanamichi*, led by a mysteriously floating candle.

Takiyasha was the daughter of the 10th-century general Taira no Masakado, who ruled supreme over eastern Japan before he was slain in 940 after rebelling against the aristocratic powers in Kyoto. Determined to avenge her father's death, Takiyasha fortifies herself with the magical power of her familiar, a toad, and disguises herself as a courtesan, wearing a gorgeous robe embroidered with cobwebs

82

39.　　Nakamura Jakuemon as Takiyasha disguised as a courtesan in *"Masakado"* (National Theater, January 1992)
Photograph by Akira Iwata

and maple leaves. She tries to bewitch Ōya Mitsukuni, an investigator sent to probe the strange goings-on at her old family mansion at Sōma in northern Chiba Prefecture, telling him, to the accompaniment of evocative Tokiwazu music, that she has fallen in love with him (fig. 39). Mitsukuni, in turn, describes the death of Takiyasha's father; and while listening to his story, Takiyasha reveals her true identity. Accompanied by the toad, she climbs on top of her ruined ancestral home and unfurls a red banner bearing the emblem of her family (fig. 38), glaring down at Mitsukuni all the while.

Tokihime in "*Kamakura Sandaiki* (Records of the Three Generations of the Kamakura Shogunate)"

40.   Nakamura Jakuemon as Tokihime (left) and Nakamura Baigyoku as Miuranosuke
      in *"Kamakura Sandaiki"*
      (Kabukiza, November 1983)
      Photograph by Yutaka Umemura

"*Kamakura Sandaiki*" is an excellent *jidaimono* adapted from Act VII of a 1781 Bunraku play set in 1204 which explores the hostile relationship between Minamoto no Yoriiye, the second of the Kamakura shoguns, and his regent Hōjō Tokimasa. Jakuemon performs Tokihime, the lovely daughter of the strongman Tokimasa, a character who is in fact modeled after the 17th-century lady Senhime, the granddaughter of Tokugawa Ieyasu. (Ieyasu established the Tokugawa shogunate in 1603 and slew Toyotomi Hideyoshi's son, Hideyori, in 1615.)

Deeply in love with Shogun Yoriiye's handsome young retainer, Miuranosuke, Tokihime has left her home and come to Kinugawa Village to take care of Miuranosuke's old mother who is critically ill. Dressed in a lavish long-sleeved kimono of brilliant red, Tokihime nurses the old woman in a thatched farmhouse —a wonderful incongruity such as is often found in *jidaimono* plays. Miuranosuke,

84

meanwhile, has been seriously wounded in battle. He makes it to his mother's house, fainting upon arrival, but he revives after Tokihime administers a dose of herb extract. His mother refuses to receive Miuranosuke, because she disapproves of his abandoning of duties for personal reasons, so he decides to return to the front without seeing her. Sensing that Miuranosuke will surely die, Tokihime entreats him to spend one night with her (fig. 40). Tokimasa's messenger, Adachi Tōzaburō, then arrives and hands Tokihime her dagger, which he has brought from her house. Tokihime reads on its blade a message from her father, Tokimasa, ordering her to kill Miuranosuke's mother and return home. Sensing that Miuranosuke suspects her, because she is the daughter of the man he is fighting against, Tokihime tries to stab herself with the dagger — but is prevented by her lover. Miuranosuke urges Tokihime to go back to her father and kill him, then kill herself, too. She promises that she will do as he commands in order to prove her loyalty to him.

Jakuemon tackled the part of Tokihime for the first time in 1956, at the age of thirty-six, after coaching by the late Nakamura Utaemon who was unrivaled in performing famous *jidaimono* heroines such as Tokihime. He has played Tokihime many times since then — as in 1983 and 1999, when he took the role opposite Nakamura Baigyoku as Miuranosuke. Jakuemon gives marvelous renditions of this beautiful, passionate young noblewoman, who becomes amazingly strong when she decides to be true to the man she loves.

Umegawa in "*Koibikyaku Yamato Ōrai* (The Couriers of Love Fleeing to Yamato)"

41. Nakamura Jakuemon as Umegawa (left) and the late Kataoka Nizaemon XIII as Magoemon in the scene titled "The Ninokuchi Village," part of "*Koibikyaku Yamato Ōrai*" (National Theater, April 1983)
   Photograph by Yutaka Umemura

"*Koibikyaku Yamato Ōrai*" is a Kabuki play adapted from Chikamatsu Monzaemon's 1711 Bunraku masterpiece, "*Meido no Hikyaku* (The Couriers of Love to the Netherworld)." The play centers on the hot-blooded Chūbei, the son of a farmer called Magoemon in Ninokuchi Village in Yamato (Nara Prefecture), who has been adopted by a merchant in Osaka in the business of dispatching couriers to transport money.

Smitten with Umegawa, a beautiful courtesan in Shinmachi, Chūbei has been spending a great deal of money on her — far beyond his means. Competing with another client for Umegawa, Chūbei even tries to buy her freedom, although he has no idea how to finance this. He has borrowed 50 *ryō* from his old friend Hachiemon to make a deposit, but has not yet been able to repay him. One day, at the Izutsuya where Umegawa works, Chūbei overhears Hachiemon abusing him in front of Umegawa and O'en, the proprietress of the house. Enraged, Chūbei confronts Hachiemon, and carried away by his eagerness to convince his friend that he has got enough money with him, he opens the packages containing 300 *ryō* that he is supposed to be delivering to a customer. Realizing that he has committed a crime that will cost him his life, Chūbei hands the money to O'en to pay for Umegawa's release. After confessing to Umegawa what he has done, he leaves, trembling, taking the courtesan with him. When they arrive in Ninokuchi Village, Umegawa helps Chūbei bid farewell to his old father, Magoemon. The play ends as Magoemon stands in the snow, watching the young couple hurry away to their doom.

"*Koibikyaku Yamato Ōrai*" is presented in the gentle, realistic *wagoto* style of Kabuki acting unique to the Kyoto-Osaka region. Jakuemon, as the kind and loving Umegawa, is shown in plate 4 with Kataoka Nizaemon in the role of Chūbei as they are about to flee from Osaka. The photograph on the facing page (fig. 41) shows Umegawa talking to Magoemon, performed by Nizaemon's deceased father, Kataoka Nizaemon XIII, who was unsurpassed in enacting such characters in the authentic *wagoto* style.

Yaegakihime in "*Honchō Nijūshikō* (The Twenty-four Models of Filial Piety: The Japanese Version)"

42. Nakamura Jakuemon as Yaegakihime in the incense-burning scene of "*Honchō Nijūshikō*" (Kabukiza, November 2002)
Photograph by Fumio Watanabe

In the scenes of "Burning Incense" and the "Inner Garden" from "*Honchō Nijūshikō*," adapted from Act IV of the 1766 Bunraku play with the same title, Jakuemon performs Yaegakihime, the beautiful, passionate daughter of the 16th-century warlord Nagao (Uesugi) Kenshin, ruler of Echigo Province (Niigata Prefecture). He performs the role in the style he learned from the late Nakamura Utaemon in 1956. Over the past half a century, Jakuemon has played Yaegakihime a great many times, most recently in November 2002. In that production, he played opposite Onoe Kikugorō as Katsuyori, the son of another noted warlord, Takeda Shingen of Kai Province (Yamanashi Prefecture). Kikugorō's performance was in the style he had inherited from his deceased father, Onoe Baikō VII.

The play begins with Yaegakihime, clad in a bright red long-sleeved kimono, mourning the death of her fiancé, Katsuyori, in her father's house at Suwa (fig. 42). Not knowing that Katsuyori's life has been spared by the sacrifice of a young man called Minosaku, Yaegakihime prays to the portrait of Katsuyori hanging in the alcove, burning incense before the picture. In another room, Nureginu, Yaegakihime's lady-in-waiting, who in fact is a spy sent from Takeda Shingen, is praying for her husband, Minosaku, who died as a substitute for Katsuyori. Katsuyori then appears, posing as an elegantly dressed gardener who has just been hired by Nagao Kenshin. Seeing Katsuyori, Nureginu weeps, remembering her husband who sacrificed himself to save Katsuyori's life. Wondering what is happening in the adjoining room, Yaegakihime looks in and finds that there is a young man who looks exactly like the portrait she has been lamenting over for days. Falling in love with the young man at first sight, Yaegakihime begs Nureginu to help her win his heart. Katsuyori keeps rejecting Yaegakihime's advances, prompting Nureginu to suggest to Yaegakihime that she steal a precious helmet hidden in her house and present it to him as a token of her love. Yaegakihime is overjoyed when she discovers that the young man is indeed Katsuyori, whom she believed to have been dead. She learns also that Katsuyori and Nureginu entered her household in disguise to steal the helmet.

The bliss of the two lovers is shattered by the sudden appearance of Nagao Kenshin, Yaegakihime's father, who sends Katsuyori away on an errand. When Yaegakihime finds that her father has sent two officers after Katsuyori to kill him, she decides instantly to help her lover by betraying her father. So she steals the helmet enshrined in the inner garden of Kenshin's residence (fig. 43) and prays fervently. Protected by a fox god inhabiting the helmet, Yaegakihime runs over the frozen water of Lake Suwa to overtake Katsuyori and help him escape his pursuers.

43.　Nakamura Jakuemon as Yaegakihime in the final scene of *"Honchō Nijūshikō"* (Kabukiza, March 1999)

Photograph by Akira Iwata

Yatsuhashi in "*Kagotsurube* (The Sword Kagotsurube)"

44.   Nakamura Kichiemon as Jirozaemon (left) and Nakamura Jakuemon as the courtesan
       Yatsuhashi at the main gate to Yoshiwara in "*Kagotsurube*"
       (Kabukiza, September 2002)
       Photograph by Shōchiku Photographic Department

Traditionally, it is essential for an *onnagata* to perform courtesans perfectly, and Yatsuhashi, in Kawatake Shinshichi's 1888 "*Kagotsurube*," is one of the most important courtesan roles in the Kabuki repertoire. When Jakuemon made his debut as Yatsuhashi in Tokyo in 1958, at the age of thirty-eight, he was coached by Nakamura Utaemon, at the time Kabuki's foremost *onnagata*—a prominence established by Utaemon's own initial performance of Yatsuhashi in 1947. In the two years following his debut in the role, Jakuemon played Yatsuhashi in Osaka and Kyoto, opposite his mentor, Ichikawa Jukai, in the lead role of Jirozaemon. After that, however, Jakuemon did not have a chance to perform this particular character for thirty-four years—until 1994, a year after Utaemon retired from the Kabuki stage owing to illness. In preparing for his undertaking in June 1994, Jakuemon was fortunate

45. Nakamura Jakuemon as Yatsuhashi, sorrowing after breaking up with Jirozaemon in "*Kagotsurube*" (Kabukiza, September 2002)

Photograph by Akira Iwata

enough to receive instruction from Utaemon, then on his sickbed, to refresh what he had first learned from the master in 1958.

"*Kagotsurube*" is the story of Jirozaemon, a pockmarked middle-aged silk merchant from Sano in Tochigi Prefecture, who is ruined by his love for Yatsuhashi, the most famous courtesan in the Yoshiwara pleasure quarters of Edo. As the naive

46.   Nakamura Jakuemon as Yatsuhashi in the final scene
of *"Kagotsurube"*
(Kabukiza, September 2002)
Photograph by Akira Iwata

but curious Jirozaemon enters the main gate to Yoshiwara, which stands under cherry trees in full bloom, he and his faithful servant, Jiroku, encounter the splendidly attired Yatsuhashi parading in state (fig. 44). As she passes Jirozaemon and reaches the edge of the *hanamichi* passageway, Yatsuhashi throws a side glance — and an enticing smile — at the dumbfounded Jirozaemon. Instantly besotted, the man begins to

47.　Nakamura Jakuemon as Yatsuhashi (left) and Nakamura Kichiemon as Jirozaemon
in the final scene of *"Kagotsurube"*
(Kabukiza, September 2002)
Photograph by Shōchiku Photographic Department

lavish money on the courtesan, finally proposing to buy her freedom and marry her.

Jirozaemon's dream is shattered, however, when Yatsuhashi tells him, in front of the two friends he has brought with him, that she does not want to see him any more because she has a steady lover (fig. 45). Humiliated, Jirozaemon retreats quietly, but returns to Yoshiwara four months later. He urges Yatsuhashi to drink sake with him, but after reminding her of his public disgrace, he kills her with a single blow from a sword named Kagotsurube, renowned for its mysterious ability to influence its owner (figs. 46 and 47). The play ends as the deranged Jirozaemon stands alone, gazing admiringly at the sword.

The photographs shown here were taken during Jakuemon's most recent performance of *"Kagotsurube"* at the Kabukiza in September 2002, with his nephew, Nakamura Kichiemon, taking the part of Jirozaemon.

Yūgiri in "*Yoshidaya*," also known as "*Kuruwa Bunshō* (A Story of the Pleasure Quarters)"

48.   Nakamura Jakuemon as the courtesan Yūgiri (left) and Nakamura Ganjirō as Izaemon
in "*Yoshidaya*"
(Meijiza, April 1993)
Photograph by Yutaka Umemura

Adapted for the Kabuki stage in 1808 from part of Chikamatsu Monzaemon's 1712 Bunraku play "*Yūgiri Awa no Naruto* (Yūgiri at Naruto)," and performed to the accompaniment of Gidayū and Tokiwazu music, the one-act "*Yoshidaya*" is simple in plot and extremely enjoyable.

Izaemon, disowned by his wealthy merchant family because of his dissipated way of life, comes to the front door of the Yoshidaya pleasure house in Osaka one New Year's Eve, wearing a woven hat of rushes to hide his face. He is anxious to see his courtesan-lover Yūgiri, whom he has not visited for some time because he had run out of money to spend on her. Following a skirmish with the manservants of the house, Izaemon is ushered into the parlor, which has been decorated for the New Year, by Kizaemon, the proprietor of the Yoshidaya. After being welcomed by Kizaemon's vivacious wife, Okisa, Izaemon waits for Yūgiri. He opens the paper-covered *fusuma* doors one after another to peep into the room where Yūgiri is supposedly preparing to see him. Instead, he sees Yūgiri entertaining another customer. Izaemon's jealousy mounts. When Yūgiri finally appears and tells him that she has been sick from not seeing him for a whole year, Izaemon, feeling cross, behaves like a spoiled child. Presently, however, the two are reconciled, and the money to buy Yūgiri's freedom is delivered from Izaemon's family.

In this marvelous photograph taken in 1993 (fig. 48), Jakuemon performs Yūgiri opposite Nakamura Ganjirō, who plays Izaemon in the gentle, sensuous *wagoto* style of acting that is unique to his family. Izaemon is dressed in a purple and black kimono known as *kamiko*, which symbolizes his impoverished state.

Yukihime in "*Kinkakuji* (The Golden Pavilion)"

49.   Nakamura Jakuemon as Yukihime in *"Kinkakuji"*
       (National Theater, November 1997)
       Photograph by Shōchiku Photographic Department

Adapted from Act IV of the 1757 Bunraku play *"Gion Sairei Shinkōki* (A Record of the Gion Festival)," *"Kinkakuji"* is a superb example of the stylized beauty of some Kabuki plays, being staged against spectacular scenery. This one-act play centers on the princely villain Matsunaga Daizen who, having destroyed Shogun Ashikaga Yoshiteru, is now holding the shogun's mother, the beautiful Yukihime, and her painter husband Kanō Naonobu, hostage at the Golden Pavilion in Kyoto. One of the three most famous princesses in *jidaimono*, Yukihime, the daughter of the renowned painter Sesson, is endowed with the exquisite charms of a mature woman, wearing a long-sleeved pink kimono. As Yukihime is an accomplished painter herself, Daizen orders her to paint a picture of a dragon on the ceiling of the pavilion. If she does not comply with his order, declares Daizen, she will have to yield to his desires.

When Yukihime discovers that her father, Sesson, was killed by Daizen, and that a precious sword belonging to her family was stolen by him, she tries to take revenge —but in vain. To punish Yukihime, Daizen has her tied to the trunk of a great cherry tree standing in the courtyard and orders that her husband, Naonobu, be beheaded. After seeing Naonobu sent to his execution, Yukihime stands helpless in a storm of cherry petals (figs. 49 and 50). Remembering what her grandfather did under similar circumstances, Yukihime first gathers a pile of cherry petals on the ground and using her right foot, manages to trace the outline of a mouse in them. Miraculously, two white mice emerge from nowhere and chew through the ropes that bind her body. Set free, Yukihime exits joyfully over the *hanamichi* to join her husband whose life has been spared by her secret ally, an elegant warrior named Konoshita Tōkichi (actually Kinoshita Tōkichirō, who was later known as the great warlord Toyotomi Hideyoshi).

Yukihime has been one of Jakuemon's favorite *jidaimono* characters ever since his thirties, when he learned how to play the role from the late Nakamura Utaemon VI. He performed Yukihime on the occasion of his succession to the stage name of Nakamura Jakuemon IV at the Kabukiza in September 1964.

50.   Nakamura Jakuemon as Yukihime
      in *"Kinkakuji"*
      (NHK Hall, February 21, 1988)
      Photograph by Akira Iwata

Postscript

It has been my great pleasure to introduce, in this book, the marvelous photographs of Nakamura Jakuemon taken over a number of decades by Yutaka Umemura. It was a desire to share Mr. Umemura's wonderful work, and my own experiences of talking with Jakuemon in his dressing room at the Kabukiza, that first led me to plan this volume. My experience of working with Jakuemon has been challenging at times, but always rewarding, and I hope that readers will consider the end result worthwhile.

In addition to Mr. Umemura, a number of people have provided invaluable assistance in the preparation of this book. I am deeply grateful to Messrs. Akira Iwata and Fumio Watanabe and members of Shōchiku Photographic Department for providing me with excellent photographs from the most recent decade of Jakuemon's career. I extend my sincere thanks also to the two important art museums in Tokyo — the Idemitsu and the Seikadō Bunko — that have generously allowed me to reproduce images of screen-paintings from their collections.

For the editing of this manuscript, I thank my friends Victoria James, Mio Yamada and Elizabeth Ingrams, members of the editorial staff on *The Japan Times*. The beautifully printed appearance of the manuscript is due to the patience and hard work of Ken'ichi Terashima, head of Ōwa Printing Company. This is the first English-language text that Mr. Terashima has ever handled, and the result of our difficult undertaking is a book that is completely "handcrafted."

It is my hope that the care and effort of all those named above has produced a book that you, the reader, have found to be enlightening and enjoyable reading.

Rei Sasaguchi
October 2004

Glossary

Ageya   House of pleasure, brothel

Akechi Mitsuhide (1528-1582)   Oda Nobunagai's vassal notorious for his rebellion against Nobunaga in 1582

Aragoto   The bombastic style of Kabuki acting originated by Ichikawa Danjūrō I in the late 17th century

Ayamegusa   Essays by Yoshizawa Ayame (1673-1729) on the art of *onnagata* acting

Bijinga   Paintings or ukiyo-e prints of beautiful women

Bon odori   Dances performed in the open at the *ullambana* festival

Dōke   Jester

Edo   The seat of the Tokugawa shogunate, renamed Tokyo in 1868

Fudō Myōō (Acalanātha)   The most powerful esoteric Buddhist deity popular in medieval Japan

Fusuma   Paper-covered sliding doors

Hanamichi   Passageway to the Kabuki stage

Hashigakari   Bridge-like structure leading to the Noh stage

Hatamoto   High-ranking samurai serving the Tokugawa shogun

Hikinuki   Technique of changing costume onstage

Hime   The daughter of someone

Jidaimono   Historical play

Kamigata   The Kyoto-Osaka region

Kata   Acting patterns

Katakiyaku   A villain's role or the actor who performs it

Keisei   High-ranking courtesan

Komai   Short pieces of *mai* dance performed in Kyōgen plays

Kouta   Love songs popular in 16th- and 17th-century Japan

Kyōgen   Mimicry-based plays that are realistic and comical; one of the traditional Japanese theaters developed in the 14th and 15th centuries

Ma   Timing

Machishū   The influential merchant classes in Kyoto and Sakai during the 15th and 16th centuries

Mai   The type of dance popular in medieval Japan, characterized by deliberate gliding or circling movements

Michiyuki   Journey

Mie   Climactic poses used in the *aragoto* acting

Monomane   Mimicry

Nagauta   The most popular type of music that developed in Edo, consisting of songs sung to the accompaniment of samisen and *tsuzumi* drums

Namban   Nickname for the Portuguese who came to Japan for trade in the 16th century

Naniwa   The classical name for Osaka

Ningyō jōruri   Puppet show (now called Bunraku)

Oda Nobunaga (1534-1582)   The famous warlord who destroyed the Ashikaga shogunate in 1573 and was assassinated by Akechi Mitsuhide in 1582

Odori   The general name for any kind of Japanese dance, apart from *mai* dance

Oie sōdō   Troubles in a daimyo's household

Onnagata   Actor performing female roles

Otokodate   Men with loyal, chivalrous spirit

Rōnin   Masterless samurai

Ryō   The gold currency used in the Tokugawa Period. 1 *ryō* is 4 *bu* or 16 *shu* and may be considered equivalent to 10,000 yen today

Sewamono   Realistic plays on the life of Edo townspeople

Shimabara   The pleasure quarters established at Suzakuno in Kyoto in 1640

Shite   Principal performer

Tachiyaku   Male lead

Terakoya   Temples or private houses where children were taught in the Tokugawa Period to read, write and calculate by priests, *rōnin* and doctors

Tokugawa Ieyasu (1542-1616)   The founder of the Tokugawa shogunate

Tokugawa Period (1603-1867)   Also called the Edo Period

Toyotomi Hideyoshi (1536-1598)   Oda Nobunaga's vassal who took control of the country after destroying Akechi Mitsuhide in 1582

Tsuzuki kyōgen   Kabuki plays with several acts

Wagoto   The gentle, sensuous and realistic style of Kabuki acting unique to the Kyoto-Osaka region

Wakashu   A young man with his forelock left unshaven

Wakashugata   Actor who performs a young man with the *wakashu* hairstyle

Waki or wakiyaku   Supporting roles or an actor performing such roles

Yarō   A man with the hair growing from the forepart of his head shaved

Yoshiwara   The pleasure quarters in Edo that started at Nihombashi Fukiyachō in 1617. After being destroyed by the great fire in 1657, its location was moved to northern Asakusa and this district became known as New Yoshiwara

四世 中村雀右衛門と女方の芸

出会い

　初めて中村雀右衛門さんにお会いしたのは、1986年6月、私がジャパンタイムズの学芸欄コラムニストとして歌舞伎座の楽屋にインタビューに伺ったおりだった。当時六十五歳だった雀右衛門さんは、女方の名優として正に絶頂期にあった。その翌年から私は出光美術館に勤めるようになったので、しばらく楽屋訪問が出来なかったが、1999年の秋、十三年ぶりにお訪ねしたときは、前と変わらない彼の若々しさに驚かされたものである。そしてその後も雀右衛門さんの舞台は好調が続き、歌舞伎座でも毎月のように大役を演じておられるのは、周知の通りである。

　本来は美術史家である私は、ジャパンタイムズに劇評を書くために二十年以上歌舞伎をみてきたのだが、数年前、人間国宝の女方・中村雀右衛門に焦点をあてて、私なりの歌舞伎観を英文でまとめてみようと思い立った。そして雀右衛門さんにお話したところ、「いつでも楽屋においで下さい」「何でも話します」とのありがたいお返事をいただいた。それから月に一、二度、歌舞伎座で雀右衛門さんの舞台を拝見する前に楽屋へ立ち寄って、化粧中の彼から、その月演じておられる役のお話を聞かせていただいたのである。

　私が中村雀右衛門という歌舞伎俳優に魅力を感じたのには、理由がある。それはまず、雀右衛門が女方一筋で兼ねることの無い役者だからである。しかも、彼が女方になろうと決心したのは非常に遅かった。中村雀右衛門は、六代目大谷友右衛門の長男として七歳で初舞台を踏み、立役として成長した。1941年、二十歳のとき軍隊に召集され、東南アジアの戦場に送られたが、幸いにも六年後に帰国した雀右衛門は、七代目松本幸四郎にすすめられ、またその後楯を得て、二十七歳にしてはじめて女方の修業を始め、以来五十余年、ひたすら「女方」に徹してこられたのである。

　中村雀右衛門の芸の本質に迫るには、まず歴史を遡って、日本における「歌舞伎」という伝統演劇の成立からその展開を通して、女方とよばれる特殊な役柄がどのような状況の下で生まれたかを辿らなければならない。そもそも歌舞伎の始まりは、「出雲のおくに」と称する女芸能者が1603年（慶長八年）の春、京都の北野天満宮で舞台にかけた「かぶき踊り」にあることは

広く知られている。おくにの「かぶき踊り」のユニークな点は、女であるおくに自身が傾いた身なりでシテ（主役）を演じ、狂言の『木六駄』に出てくるような茶屋の主人を女主人にして、男の狂言師に演じさせたことである。ちなみに狂言の『若菜』では、立衆とよばれる人物が大勢あらわれて、主人公と酒を酌み交わし小舞を舞ったりするが、おくにの「かぶき踊り」では、当世風に伊達ないでたちをした客 ── つまり「かぶき者」── が茶屋の女主人と杯を交わしながら、謡の代りに小歌をうたい、小舞の代りに踊りを踊ったのである。おくには、手近にあった狂言のかたちを借りて「かぶき踊り」を仕立てたのだが、その奇抜なアイディアが京の観衆を喜ばせたのであろう。

　「かぶき踊り」で一世を風靡したおくにが1613年頃京都から姿を消した後も、「かぶき踊り」は、都の内外で数多くの女芸人や遊女によって演じ続けられた。そして女たちの「かぶき踊り」が、1629年、幕府によって禁じられてからは、若衆髷の若者たちが女の姿で登場するようになった。彼らは主として、すぐれた容色と美声、舞や踊りの技術を売り物にして人気を博したのだが、女性たちのそれと同じく風紀上の弊害が大きかったので、1652年には禁止された。翌年からは、前髪を剃り落として野郎頭となった役者たちが、「物真似狂言尽し」だけを舞台にかけるという条件で生きのびたが、1660年代に「続き狂言」が展開する上で女の役は無くてはならなかったので、男性が女方としてその役を専門に演じることになった。

　元禄期（1688～1704年）に独自の演劇形態としてめざましい発展をみせた歌舞伎は、十八世紀には江戸と上方で最盛期を迎えた。十八世紀前半に活躍した女方には芳沢あやめと初代瀬川菊之丞がいるが、彼らが女方としての芸を完成するためにした修業の仕方は、近世から現代にかけて活躍した歌舞伎の女方に受け継がれている。（芳沢あやめの書き残した『あやめぐさ』によると、女方とは正に男が舞台の上で女になることであった。そしてあやめは、役の「女」になりきるために、寝ても覚めてもその演じ方を工夫したという。）中村雀右衛門はかねがね、「芸の上では、瀬川菊之丞にまで遡ることになろうか」といっているが、彼は、三世紀も前に女方として活躍した役者を手本として修業を続けたわけである。雀右衛門が二十七歳ではじめ

て女方をめざそうと決心したとき、後に岳父となった七代目松本幸四郎に、女方として一人前になるのに三十年はかかるだろうといわれたそうだが、七代目の予測通り三十年経って大成した雀右衛門は、その後さらに二十年以上も花を咲かせ続けているのである。

　十九世紀後半から二十世紀に名声を馳せた女方としては、五世中村歌右衛門とその息子の六世中村歌右衛門があげられるが、六世歌右衛門の存在は、雀右衛門の女方の芸の形成に欠くことのできないものであった。特に時代物の代表的キャラクターである三姫（『鎌倉三代記』の時姫、『本朝廿四孝』の八重垣姫、『金閣寺』の雪姫)、『熊谷陣屋』の相模や『加賀見山旧錦絵』の尾上、さらに『寺子屋』の千代の演技技術は、まさしく歌右衛門から受け継いだものである。その歌右衛門が1993年から歌舞伎の舞台に立たなくなってから、雀右衛門は、歌右衛門に習った型を外れることなく、徐々に歌右衛門の影響から離れて、雀右衛門独自の味、あでやかな風情をみせるようになった。ここ数年にわたる雀右衛門の舞台姿は、研ぎ澄まされた、それでいてどことなくあたたか味のある美しさで、しかも神経の行き届いたその演技には、驚くような気迫がこもっている。

　このごろになって、ようやく幸せを感じるようになったとおっしゃる雀右衛門さんであるが、読者の方々にも、この書を通して、雀右衛門の半世紀にわたる努力のたまものである女方の芸にふれ、雀右衛門の舞台のきらめき、年齢を超えた瑞々しさを味わっていただければ幸いである。

中村雀右衛門
の芸の成立ち

　中村雀右衛門（本名・青木清治）は、今日活躍している歌舞伎役者としては非常に珍しく、第二次世界大戦に応召して六年間兵役に服した経歴を持つ。女性の美しさを体現する雀右衛門の舞台を見るとき、その昔、彼が東南アジアでトラック隊の軍曹であった頃の姿を誰が想像することができようか。雀右衛門は、歌舞伎役者であった六代目大谷友右衛門の長男として、七歳のときに広太郎の名で初舞台を踏み、天才子役の名を欲しいままにした。友右衛門は、息子を歌舞伎役者にふさわしく育てるために、義太夫の語り、日本舞踊、長唄や鳴り物の稽古、トンボ切りの練習、茶道の作法など、様々な素養を早くから身につけさせた。

　雀右衛門は二十歳で召集され南方へ派遣されたが、奇跡的にも、二十六歳のとき無事スマトラで終戦を迎えた。1946年に復員したが、その頃、荒廃した東京で歌舞伎はすでに復活の兆しを見せ、東劇と三越劇場で上演されていた。雀右衛門は帰国すると直ぐ、東京で当時歌舞伎界の筆頭格であった七代目松本幸四郎のもとへ行き、役者としての道を歩み直したいという希望を述べたところ、女方になるよう勧められた。雀右衛門はさらに尾上松緑を訪れたが、驚いたことに、松緑も女方になるよう助言したのである。歌舞伎役者としては中年にあたる二十七歳から女方としての厳しい修業の途につくことは、それ自体がたいへんな冒険であった。しかし雀右衛門が将来のために考えられるもうひとつの道は、戦時中の経験を生かして、自動車整備工にでもなることであった。終戦直後は、誰もが何かにしがみついて生きていかねばならない混乱の時期であったが、雀右衛門は七代目幸四郎の後楯を得て、女方になることを終生の目標に据えた。やがて雀右衛門は幸四郎の勧めで、のちに東京の歌舞伎界で女方としては並ぶもののない地位についた六世中村歌右衛門（当時芝翫）に、教えを乞うようになったのである。

　雀右衛門が戦後の歌舞伎界を生き抜きながら、究極の目標を追い求めた過程を見ることは、彼が女方としていかに成功したかを評価する上での助けとなろう。雀右衛門は地方巡業をこなすうちに、次第に女方としての経験を重ねていった。1947年、東京の三越劇場で『毛谷村』の女主人公お園を演じたとき、女方としての将来性を認められ、翌年、亡父大谷友右衛門の名跡

を継いだ。同年、雀右衛門は七代目幸四郎の長女晃子と結婚し、幸四郎の優秀な三人の息子（のちの十一代目市川團十郎、初代松本白鸚、二代目尾上松緑）とも縁続きとなるに及んで、歌舞伎界での地盤を不動のものにした。

　戦後の生活は、歌舞伎役者にとっても困難なものであった。雀右衛門も家族を養うため、1950年に東宝の歴史もの映画への出演に踏み切った。まず『佐々木小次郎』で、雀右衛門は十七世紀初頭に活躍した剣豪の佐々木小次郎を演じて一躍スターとなり、それから数年の間に三十本の映画に主演した。しかし雀右衛門は、映画製作にかかわっていた歳月を振り返って、監督の指示のままに動かねばならないことに対して言い知れぬ違和感を覚えたと言う。歌舞伎役者である雀右衛門は、歌舞伎の型や演技の規範はそれぞれの家に伝わるものではあるが、一旦習得した上は、その蓄積を踏まえて自在に演じる方が良いと考える。舞台に上がれば、自分を律する主人公は自分だからである。

　1955年、雀右衛門は一旦東京の歌舞伎の舞台に戻ったが、大阪での歌舞伎に参加するため、すぐに大阪入りをした。大阪での歌舞伎は、1958年に現地の歌舞伎座が閉館するほど衰退の一途を辿りつつあったが、幸いにも、当時大阪の歌舞伎界で指導者的立場にあった市川壽海がすぐ雀右衛門の後楯となり、その後十年近くも、相手役として雀右衛門に重要な女方の役を演じさせたのである。この偉大な役者に師事している間に、雀右衛門は徐々にレパートリーを広げ、東京に復帰する準備を進めた。

　1964年、オリンピックの年に東京に戻った彼は、そこで四世中村雀右衛門を襲名した。中村雀右衛門の名跡は、本来は三世雀右衛門の息子（中島章景）が継ぐはずであったが、幼少から仲の良かったその人はすでに戦死していたのである。襲名のおりに雀右衛門が演じた二つの女方の役のうち、『金閣寺』の雪姫の演技は特筆すべきものであった。それが先代中村雀右衛門の得意とする役の一つであったというだけでなく、戦後外地から帰った彼が東京で最初に見た芝居が、『金閣寺』であったからである。中村雀右衛門襲名に際して、雀右衛門は長男に立役の大谷友右衛門を、次男に女方の中村芝雀を、それぞれにゆかりの名跡を継がせた。

　目を覚ましている間、雀右衛門の念頭にあるのは舞台だけだ

そうである。舞台に集中するために、彼は二十年以上も前から、大好きなトラックやオートバイのみならず、自家用車を運転することも止めてしまった。そして雀右衛門が舞台で見せるのは、並外れた美しさである。しかしながらそれは、過去五十年間の努力の結晶とも言える高度に工夫された美しさで、舞台での彼の動きと声の使い方は、すべて綿密な計算の上に成り立っている。間の取り方が巧みで、言葉を発する前に一瞬息を詰めるコツは、若いときに受けた義太夫の稽古を通して培われたものに他ならない。

　雀右衛門の女方としての芸の神髄は、1984年3月、歌舞伎座で演じた『金閣寺』の雪姫の演技に見られた。鴇色（ときいろ）の衣裳を身にまとって桜の木につながれた雀右衛門は、官能的な姿態で、舞台一面に散った桜の花びらを足でまさぐりながら鼠の絵を描く。またそのすばらしい演技力は、十九世紀に書かれた世話物にも発揮される。1986年3月に歌舞伎座で上演された『源氏店』のお富の演技が、そのよい例であろう。この種類の世話物の演技の仕方は、雀右衛門がかつて歌舞伎の生字引といわれた尾上梅朝（六世尾上梅幸の弟子）から学んだものである。

　雀右衛門は、古典的な歌舞伎に通暁している女方として、歌舞伎役者がそれぞれの家に伝わる演技の基礎的な技術の習得に勤めなければならないのは無論であるが、実際に演じる場合には、いまの観客の共感を呼ぶような演技をしなければならないと信じている。雀右衛門はまた、将来、女方がより一層重要な役を演じられるような歌舞伎作品がつくられることを望んでいる。

　雀右衛門は、舞台の前に顔をつくり衣裳をつけると、見事に変身する。そして舞台では、魅力的な演技と台詞の言廻しを通して、驚くほどの若さと新鮮さを発揮する。特に自分より若くてハンサムな立役と競演するときには、それが如実に表れる。若さと新鮮さを保つために、雀右衛門は長い間スポーツジムに通って心身の鍛練を続け、常に健康管理には注意を払っている。

　雀右衛門にとって、女方を演じるということは、女らしさを抑制の効いた美しさに結晶させるという並々ならぬ過程を意味する。したがって、翌日のエネルギーを補充するために、仕事を終えた後はくつろいで気分転換を図る必要があるが、雀右衛

門はその切り換えが上手な人と言えよう。劇場に入り、楽屋の暖簾をくぐると、空気が一変するのを感じると言う。幼少の頃、騎手かカウボーイになりたかったという雀右衛門は、最近まで気ばらしのために乗馬を楽しんだ。馬に乗っていると、気分が高揚するのであろう。高いところへ登るのが好きで、冗談に、東京タワーの鉄骨を洗う仕事がしてみたかったともいう。彼はまたお洒落で有名であるが、人目を引く衣服の多くはすべて友人からの贈り物で、そのなかには著名なデザイナーも含まれている。しかし一旦贈られたものを着始めてみると、大胆な格好をすることが面白く思えるようになったらしい。「歌舞伎」という名称は、「かぶく」（傾く）という動詞に語源を発している。「かぶく」には、異様な身なりをする、或いは人目につく衣裳を身につけるという意味があるから、雀右衛門は歌舞伎スタイルを装おうことによって、真に歌舞伎の精神を具現化しているといえよう。

　先週のある日、私が歌舞伎座の楽屋を訪れたとき、丁度舞台を終えた雀右衛門はオレンジ色の部屋着に着替え、ファンから贈られた花に囲まれて、美しい鏡台の前に座ってくつろいでいたが、その姿からは、自由で屈託のない、心の広い人となりが感じられた。また優しくて、こまやかな心遣いを見せる人でもある。そのような雀右衛門が、戦争から無事生還して女方になり、今もなお歌舞伎界の大切な財産として舞台に立っておられることに、心から喝采をおくりたいと思う。

（1986年 6 月21日ジャパンタイムズ掲載）

<h1>【中村雀右衛門の得意とする役と上演リスト】</h1>

15. 「隅田川」の斑女の前

中村富十郎の舟人

（2000年 3 月　歌舞伎座）

16. 「隅田川」の斑女の前

中村富十郎の舟人

（2000年 3 月　歌舞伎座）

17. 「隅田川」の斑女の前

（2000年 3 月　歌舞伎座）

18. 「十六夜清心」の十六夜
（いざよいせいしん）

尾上菊五郎の清心

（1979年 5 月　歌舞伎座）

19. 「かさね」（色彩間苅豆）のかさね
（いろもようちょっとかりまめ）

（1999年 4 月　歌舞伎座）

20. 「かさね」（色彩間苅豆）のかさね

中村吉右衛門の与右衛門

（1999年 4 月　歌舞伎座）

21. 「かさね」（色彩間苅豆）のかさね

（1999年 4 月　歌舞伎座）

22. 「二人椀久」の松山
（ににんわんきゅう）

（2000年 9 月　歌舞伎座）

23. 「二人椀久」の松山

中村富十郎の椀久

（2000年 9 月　歌舞伎座）

24. 「妹背山婦女庭訓・道行」のお三輪
（いもせやまおんなていきん）

尾上菊五郎の求女と中村芝翫の橘姫

（1988年 5 月　歌舞伎座）

25. 「妹背山婦女庭訓・御殿」のお三輪

（1998年11月　歌舞伎座）

26. 「加賀見山旧錦絵」の尾上
（かがみやまこきょうのにしきえ）

（1990年 6 月　歌舞伎座）

27. 「加賀見山旧錦絵」の尾上

（1994年 9 月　歌舞伎座）

28. 「夏祭浪花鑑」のお辰
（なつまつりなにわかゞみ）

中村富十郎の三婦
（さぶ）

（1993年 9 月　歌舞伎座）

29. 「夏祭浪花鑑」のお辰

（1999年 6 月　歌舞伎座）

30. 「吃又」（傾城反魂香）のおとく
（どもまた）（けいせいはんごんこう）

中村吉右衛門の又平

（1991年 9 月　歌舞伎座）

31. 「吃又」（傾城反魂香）のおとく

３代目実川延若の又平

（1978年11月　歌舞伎座）

32. 「源氏店」（与話情浮名横櫛）のお富
（よわなさけうきなのよこぐし）

（1974年12月　帝国劇場）

33. 「源氏店」（与話情浮名横櫛）のお富

（1974年12月　帝国劇場）

34. 「熊谷陣屋」（一谷嫩軍記）の相模
（いちのたにふたばぐんき）

（1987年10月　歌舞伎座）

35. 「鳴神」の雲の絶間姫

中村吉右衛門の鳴神上人

（1993年 1 月　歌舞伎座）

36. 「鳴神」の雲の絶間姫

市川團十郎の鳴神上人

（1986年 8 月　公立文化施設協会）

112

37. 「鳴神」の中村吉右衛門演じる鳴神上人

　　　　　（1980年1月　浅草公会堂）

38. 「将門」（忍夜恋曲者）の滝夜叉姫

　　　市川團十郎の大宅光圀

　　　　　（1992年1月　国立劇場）

39. 「将門」（忍夜恋曲者）の滝夜叉姫

　　　　　（1992年1月　国立劇場）

40. 「鎌倉三代記」の時姫

　　　中村梅玉の三浦之助

　　　　　（1983年11月　歌舞伎座）

41. 「恋飛脚大和往来・新口村の場」の梅川

　　　13代目片岡仁左衛門の孫右衛門

　　　　　（1983年4月　国立劇場）

42. 「本朝廿四孝・十種香」の八重垣姫

　　　　　（2002年11月　歌舞伎座）

43. 「本朝廿四孝・奥庭」の八重垣姫

　　　　　（1999年3月　歌舞伎座）

44. 「籠釣瓶花街酔醒・吉原仲之町見染の場」
　　の八ッ橋

　　　中村吉右衛門の次郎左衛門

　　　　　（2002年9月　歌舞伎座）

45. 「籠釣瓶花街酔醒・縁切りの場」の八ッ橋

　　　　　（2002年9月　歌舞伎座）

46. 「籠釣瓶花街酔醒・立花屋二階の場」の
　　八ッ橋

　　　　　（2002年9月　歌舞伎座）

47. 「籠釣瓶花街酔醒・立花屋二階の場」の
　　八ッ橋

　　　中村吉右衛門の次郎左衛門

　　　　　（2002年9月　歌舞伎座）

48. 「吉田屋」（廓文章）の夕霧

　　　中村鴈治郎の伊左衛門

　　　　　（1993年4月　明治座）

49. 「金閣寺」（祇園祭礼信仰記）の雪姫

　　　　　（1997年11月　国立劇場）

50. 「金閣寺」（祇園祭礼信仰記）の雪姫

　　　　　（1988年2月21日　NHKホール）

113

この本の刊行
にあたって

　中村雀右衛門さんを英文で紹介する本をつくるということは、予想以上に難しい仕事でした。はじめは、主に歌舞伎に興味を持っておられる外国の読者を対象に考えていたのですが、本がかたちになっていくうちに、日本の歌舞伎ファンの方々にも愉しんでいただけるようにしたいと考え出したからです。

　本書の前半は、歌舞伎の誕生と初期の展開、女の役を専門に演じる歌舞伎役者がどのような状況に生まれ、その芸がどのように形成されたかについての英文論考からなります。雀右衛門さんが伝統的な女方の演技技術を継承して大成させた過程は、1986年6月21日、ジャパンタイムズに掲載されたインタビューの記事で見ていただくことにしました。日本の読者のためには、「まえがき」に当る部分を雀右衛門さんとの「出会い」として、「中村雀右衛門の芸の成立ち」と題したジャパンタイムズの記事の日本語訳とともに巻末に加えてみました。

　本書の最大の魅力はその後半にあって、中村雀右衛門の歌舞伎レパートリーから選んだ21演目の筋を、すばらしい舞台写真をつかって紹介していることです。梅村豊氏が長年にわたって撮影した雀右衛門さんの写真にはストーリー性に富んだすぐれたものが多く、知られざる「雀右衛門の世界」の魅力を味わうことができます。他に松竹写真部、岩田アキラ氏、渡辺文雄氏にも、それぞれ立派な写真を提供していただきました。また本文に載せるため、出光美術館と静嘉堂文庫美術館からも所蔵品の写真を拝借できましたので、ここに厚く御礼申し上げます。

　この書は、本文をはじめとして、校正刷りのチェック、レイアウトから装訂まで、すべて私の手づくりの作品ですが、応和印刷株式会社の寺島研一氏が長い間辛抱強く付き合ってくださったお蔭で、ようやく出版の運びにいたりました。なおこの本の刊行を実現させる上で相談にのっていただいた方には、梅村氏のほかに東京大学名誉教授の原実氏がおられます。インド哲学ご専門の原先生は若いときから歌舞伎愛好家なので、同氏の助言は非常に役に立ちました。また英文原稿の編集に協力してくださったジャパンタイムズ勤務のヴィクトリア・ジェイムスさんと山田みをさんはもちろんのこと、遠くオックスフォードから応援して下さった友人のアン・ハリース夫人にも、心から感謝の意を表したいと思います。

2004年10月

笹　口　　玲

四世　中村雀右衛門
―― 時を超える情熱と美

制　　作　　応和印刷株式会社

編集・発行　　笹口　玲
　　　　　　　東京都港区麻布台一―一一―一九―六〇二

著　　者　　笹口　玲

発行日　　平成十六年十月

Nakamura Jakuemon IV
The Art of *Onnagata* Acting

Designed and published by the author, Rei Sasaguchi.
Edited by Victoria James, Mio Yamada and Elizabeth Ingrams.
Typography by Nitta Planning, Tokyo.
Printed and bound by Ōwa Printing Co., Ltd., Tokyo, 2004.

ISBN4-9902185-0-7